To Jan

Table of Contents

Abbreviations

AER	*American Ecclesiastical Review*
AnBib	Analecta Biblica
ASNU	Acta seminarii neotestamentici upsaliensis
BAGD	W. Bauer, W.F. Arndt, F.W. Gingrich, and F. Danker, eds., *A Greek-English Lexicon of the New Testament and Other Early Christian Literature* (Chicago: University of Chicago, 1969)
BHT	Beiträge zur historischen Theologie
BTB	*Biblical Theology Bulletin*
CBQ	*Catholic Biblical Quarterly*
CBQMS	Catholic Biblical Quarterly Monograph Series
ExpTim	*Expository Times*
GBS	Guides to Biblical Scholarship Series
HTKNT	Herders Theologischer Kommentar zum Nuen Testament
IB	*Interpreter's Bible* (Nashville: Abingdon, 1952)
IDB	*Interpreter's Dictionary of the Bible* (Nashville: Abingdon, 1962)
Int	*Interpretation*
JBL	*Journal of Biblical Literature*

JBR	*Journal of Bible and Religion*
JR	*Journal of Religion*
JSNTSup	Journal for the Study of the New Testament—Supplement Series
JTS	*Journal of Theological Studies*
NovT	*Novum Testamentum*
NovTSup	Novum Testamentum, Supplements
NTS	*New Testament Studies*
PRS	*Perspectives In Religious Studies*
RevExp	*Review and Expositor*
SANT	Studien zum Alten und Neuen Testament
SBLDS	Society of Biblical Literature Dissertation Series
SBLMS	Society of Biblical Literature Monograph Series
SBS	Stuttgarter Bibelstudien
SBT	Studies in Biblical Theology
SNTSMS	Studiorum Novi Testamenti Societas, Monograph Series
ST	*Studia Theologica*
TBT	*The Bible Today*
TD	*Theology Digest*
TDNT	G. Kittel and G. Friedrich, eds., *Theological Dictionary of the New Testament* (10 vols.; Grand Rapids: Eerdmans, 1964-1976)
TTS	Trier Theologische Studien
ZNW	*Zeitschrift für die neutestamentliche Wissenschaft*

Introduction

What does it mean to be a disciple of Jesus Christ? What does "following" Jesus entail in terms of one's daily life? This book looks at how the author of Mark's Gospel answers these questions. As we examine Mark's narrative it will become clear that discipleship is one of his most important themes. Mark tells his readers what it means to "follow" Jesus not only in the stories and the discipleship discourses, but throughout the Gospel. The recognition that there is a communal dimension to discipleship will lead us into a discussion of the place of the Eucharist and baptism in the life of the Christian. We will see that prayer is an important element of discipleship, and that "following" Jesus has radical implications for one's attitude toward possessions. In the end, however, one's understanding of discipleship and one's ability to follow as a disciple are directly dependent on one's understanding of Jesus. Thus we will be led to discuss Christology and its relationship to discipleship. According to Mark, the nature of discipleship becomes clear only in the light of the cross. This means that one must understand Jesus as the Suffering Servant who is the Son of God. Jesus came "to serve, not to be served"; the Christian disciple must, therefore, adopt a lifestyle that follows Jesus' example of service to all.

This book is directed to the informed and educated general reader as well as to the college theology student. Although not primarily written for the specialized scholarly community, I believe that it also will be of use to this constituency.

My professional interest in Christian discipleship began in the early 1970s when I had the privilege of studying with Dr. Werner H. Kelber at the University of Dayton. It grew and developed at the University of Notre Dame under the guidance of Dr. Elisabeth Schüssler Fiorenza. To both these scholars I owe an undying debt of gratitude.

Research for this volume began in 1985 and was made possible by a Saint Anselm College Summer Research Grant. I would like to thank the members of the Grant Review Committee and the Governing Board of the College for their confidence and support. A debt of gratitude is also owed to Fr. Peter J. Guerin, O.S.B., Dean of the College; Dr. James McGhee, chair of the Theology Department; and my colleagues in the Theology Department for their support and encouragement over the years. The members of the faculty and staff of Saint Anselm College as well as the students in my classes also deserve my thanks for their thought provoking questions which have assisted me in presenting my positions more carefully.

My special thanks are due to several good friends who read over the entire manuscript, Bob and Lorry Roy of Goffstown, NH, for their helpful comments, and Dr. Patrick F. O'Connell of Villa Maria College for his valuable stylistic and exegetical suggestions. Their assistance has resulted in numerous improvements; any remaining errors are my responsibility.

Finally, I would like to express my indebtedness to my wife, Jan, and my children, Susan and Karen. Without their support this book could not have been written.

1

Call Stories

In trying to determine what it means to follow Jesus, the most obvious place to start is with the call stories, those pericopes (passages, stories) where Jesus explicitly calls people to follow him and they respond positively or negatively. In examining these stories we will discover what the initial call to become a disciple of Jesus entailed.

The structure of Mark's Gospel as a whole indicates that discipleship is an important concern of the author. It has been pointed out more than once that discipleship pericopes inaugurate every major section of the Gospel.[1] When one looks more closely at this overall structure, one realizes that it is in fact call and commissioning stories that begin the first three major sections: the call of the first disciples (1:16-20), the selection of the Twelve (3:13-19), and the missionary charge to the Twelve (6:7-13).

Prior to the call of the first disciples, however, we find several verses usually referred to as the "Introduction" to Mark's Gospel. Here the author deals with the ministry of

---

[1]See E. Schweizer, "The Portrayal of the Life of Faith in the Gospel of Mark," *Int* 32 (1978) 387-399 and N. Perrin, *The New Testament: An Introduction* (2nd rev. ed. N. Perrin and D.C. Duling; New York: Harcourt, Brace, Jovanovich, 1982) 243-254.

John the Baptist, the baptism and temptation of Jesus, and the arrest of John. With the preliminaries taken care of, and the ministy of Jesus clearly separated from that of John by the latter's arrest, Jesus speaks for the first time in Mark's Gospel.

Regardless of whether 1:14-15 is seen as the conclusion of the introduction[2] or a transitional summary,[3] it is important for Mark's understanding of Jesus and discipleship. Literary criticism tells us that the first time we meet a character, the words he/she speaks are important for the reader's understanding of that character.

When the Markan Jesus first speaks, in 1:14-15, he announces the arrival of the Kingdom of God and summons the people to "repent and believe in the gospel." Mark presents this as part of Jesus' basic message addressed to all those who heard his preaching. Repenting and believing in the Gospel are seen as the appropriate responses to Jesus' announcement of the arrival of the reign of God. Mark's use of the imperative here underlines the importance and seriousness with which one should view these words of Jesus. What "repent and believe in the gospel" means is clearer when we examine the words μετάνοια (repentance) and πίστις (faith). In a general sense, μετάνοια involves a radical conversion from all that is evil and a total commitment to God. It is unconditional, once-for-all, affects the entire person, and is addressed to all without distinction.[4] The positive side of this complete commitment to the will of God is faith. πίστις implies obedience, trust, and hope as well as the acceptance of the "good news."[5]

What one understands to be the content of the "gospel" or "good news" depends on where one stands. The Galilean audience that Jesus is pictured as addressing in Mark 1:15,

---

[2] See L.E. Keck, "The Introduction to Mark's Gospel," *NTS* 12 (1966) 352-370, who argues against the widely held position that Mark's introduction consists of 1:1-13. He believes that the proper designation of the introduction is 1:1-15. The call story in 1:16-20, then, would inaugurate the gospel as Mark understands it.

[3] Perrin, *The New Testament,* 244.

[4] J. Behm, "μετανοέω and μετάνοια," *TDNT* 4, 1002.

[5] R. Bultmann, "πιστεύω," *TDNT* 6, 208.

would have understood this to include, at least, Jesus' news that the reign of God was at hand and, probably also, his teaching concerning the will of God (i.e., how one ought to conduct one's life now that the reign of God had arrived). The original readers or hearers of Mark's Gospel, however, would undoubtedly have seen this "good news" as including the early Christian preaching about Jesus, the Christ. The acceptance of the message of and about Jesus follows from the complete turnabout in life Jesus demands.

The center around which this repenting and believing revolves is the $\beta\alpha\sigma\iota\lambda\epsilon\iota\alpha$ of God." Although it is usually translated as "kingdom," $\beta\alpha\sigma\iota\lambda\epsilon\iota\alpha$ refers to the activity of ruling and can be translated as "reign of God" (e.g., *New American Bible*). The people of Israel believed that the kingship of God was eternal and universal, but their experience in the world had taught them that God's rule was not universally recognized and obeyed. This apparent contradiction was resolved by the teaching that while God's sovereignty is absolute, it will be manifest in this world only in the future. Israel expected that after a final world-ending display of divine power, God's eternal and absolute rule would be mainfest and individuals would lead their lives in accordance with the will of God.

Mark tells us that instead of the final world-ending event that Israel expected, the reign of God has come in the person and ministry of Jesus. The arrival and present reality of the Kingdom is the ground of Jesus' ministry. Everything Jesus or Mark says must be understood in this light. Although the reign of God is breaking into history, the Kingdom has not yet manifested itself in its fullness. Since Jesus sometimes speaks about the approaching rule of God (e.g., 9:1), God's reign also has a future dimension. It is in this in-between time, between the "already and not yet" of the Kingdom, that Christians from Mark's day to our own live out their existence.

The precise nature of the Kingdom's presence is seen in Jesus' speech about the mystery of the Kingdom (4:3-32).[6] In

---

[6]W.H. Kelber, *The Kingdom in Mark: A New Place and A New Time* (Philadelphia: Fortress, 1974) 25-43.

the so-called "parables of growth" we learn that the reign of God is present yet hidden. There is a contrast between the present seemingly insignificant beginning of God's rule and its triumphant advent in the future. The process which will lead eventually to the coming of God's reign in its fullness, however, is already in progress. God is in control of human history and will decide when the Kingdom will come in its fullness.[7]

The inbreaking of the rule of God means that the old era has ended. A radical alternative to the former order of things now presents itself. Individuals can submit to the will of God by following the way of Jesus, which includes leading one's life in accordance with the values of the Kingdom and participating in the new type of human community made possible by its arrival.

The Call of the First Disciples (1:16-20)

[16]And passing along by the Sea of Galilee, he saw Simon and Andrew the brother of Simon casting a net in the sea; for they were fishermen. [17]And Jesus said to them, "Follow me and I will make you become fishers of men." [18]And immediately they left their nets and followed him. [19]And going on a little farther, he saw James the son of Zebedee and John his brother, who were in their boat mending the nets. [20]And immediately he called them; and they left their father Zebedee in the boat with the hired servants, and followed him.

Jesus' general call for conversion and belief (1:15) leads immediately to his much more particularized call of the first disciples (1:16-20). While there is a close connection between the first two sayings of Jesus (1:15; 1:17), it should be pointed

---

[7]See J. Jeremias, *The Parables of Jesus* (rev. ed. trans. S. Hooke; New York: Scribner's, 1963) 13ff., and N.A. Dahl, "The Parables of Growth," *ST* 5 (1952) 132-166.

out that the phrasing and connotations are quite different. The first (1:15) presents the call as repentance and faith, the second (1:17) as following and being "fishers of men." The first focuses on the Kingdom as the content of the good news, the second on personal attachment to the person of Jesus. While both calls invite individuals to participate in the present reign of God, only the latter is explicitly a call to Christian discipleship. Everyone is called to participate in the reign of God, but only some are called to be followers of Jesus.

Several comments are in order: (1) The church and the Kingdom are not identical. The church serves as the sign and instrument of God's reign as it attempts to live out its own life as a community in accordance with the will of God. (2) The order of these sayings does not mean that there is no need for Christians to repent and believe. When Jesus calls individuals to himself, he is inviting them to confront God. Repentance and faith are not acts of preparation for the Kingdom or for a personal relationship with Jesus; they are the consequences of the arrival of the reign of God in the person and works of Jesus. Such an encounter with Jesus will inevitably lead the individual to repentance and faith. (3) The missionary task, being "fishers of men," includes the call to repentance of 1:15 (cf. 6:12) and belongs properly to those who have been called by Jesus to be his disciples. (4) As pointed out above, Mark's initial readers would have understood the content of the "good news," preached as part of the missionary enterprise, to include the preaching about Jesus as well as the preaching of Jesus.

Although Mark realizes that ultimately it is participation in the reign of God which is essential for salvation, because he is writing to a Christian audience, he is interested in clearly presenting what it means to be a follower of Jesus. This particularized call to discipleship is issued to Simon, Andrew, James, and John, four Galilean fishermen, when Jesus asks them to join him on his way. Jesus calls these four individuals as he is "passing along by the Sea of Galilee" (1:16). Although the motif of "the way" is most prominent in the central section of the Gospel (8:22–10:52) it should be noted here that Jesus' calling of these disciples while he is journeying and his later call of Levi "as he passed on" (2:14) fit in well with this motif. Discipleship seems to be dynamic and not static, to involve mobility.[8]

The initiative in this first call story, as later in 2:14, is taken by Jesus. These fishermen whom Jesus encountered as he made his way along the shore of the Sea of Galilee were not seeking to join him. In fact, they do not appear to have been seeking anything. When Jesus met them they were simply engaged in tasks which were considered part of their occupations, casting or mending their fishing nets. Similarly, when Jesus came to call Levi, he found Levi busy with his duties as a tax collector. Mark appears to be making a point here about God's unexpected grace.[9]

It is not surprising that this incident puzzles many readers of Mark's Gospel. After all, there is no indication that these fishermen had heard Jesus' preaching, or undergone any special training or instruction that would have prepared them for this call. They are not presented as holier than other people. As a matter of fact, Levi, called later in 2:13-17, is engaged in an occupation considered despicable by first century Judaism.[10] What we should remember here is that throughout the Bible, God chooses to work through specific individuals and groups (e.g., Israel, the church) to accomplish his purposes. The timing of God's call and the state of the person chosen often appear puzzling to the reader. Why choose a crafty deceitful twin (Jacob), the son of a slave (Moses), a prostitute (Rahab), or a widow from Moab (Ruth)?

God seems to address his call to ordinary people as they go about their daily lives. This invitation is not something one earns, but comes freely from God. Men and women, usually seen as unlikely candidates by the reader, are chosen by God, not because they are already holier than others, but in hopes

---

[8]See J. Donaldson, "'Called to Follow,' A Twofold Experience of Discipleship in Mark," *BTB* 5 (1975) 69, and Schweizer, "Portrayal," 393-94.

[9]Schweizer, "Portrayal," 390.

[10]B.J. Bamberger, "Tax Collector," *IDB* 4, 522.

that they will cooperate with God for the successful accomplishment of God's will. This call of the first disciples, in Mark 1:16-20, highlights the gratuitous nature of God's call and the response required from the one called.

The manner in which Jesus selects his disciples stands in stark contrast to the way in which individuals became the disciples of rabbis in first century Palestine. The Jewish model, common at the time of Jesus, was one in which a prospective student would choose a rabbi to study with and would become a disciple only after much training.[11] Jesus, however, takes the initiative and calls these first disciples to follow him and to become "fishers of men."

Many readers of the New Testament uncritically assume that the relationship between Jesus and his disciples is best understood as modeled after the relationship between a rabbi and his students.[12] This conclusion has been widely challenged in scholarly circles,[13] however, and is not the best first-century Jewish model of "following" and discipleship available for understanding Christian discipleship. Of the many differences between the rabbi/student and Jesus/disciple models,[14] the most telling involves the passing on of the master's words. The most characteristic feature of the Gospel tradition, in contrast with the Jewish rabbinic tradition, is the remarkable freedom which the transmitters of the Jesus tradition exercise.[15] Thus, it cannot be maintained that Jesus required his disciples to

[11]K.H. Rengstorf, "$\mu\alpha\theta\eta\tau\acute{\eta}\varsigma$," *TDNT* 4, 444ff., and J. Neusner, *First Century Judaism in Crisis* (Nashville: Abingdon, 1975) 95-114.

[12]This position also has its scholarly advocates. See H.D. Betz, *Nachfolge und Nachahmung Jesu Christi im Neuen Testament* (BHT 37; Tübingen: Mohr/Siebeck, 1967) 27-43; B. Gerhardsson, *Memory and Manuscript* (ASNU 22; Lund: Gleerup, 1961); and K.H. Rengstorf, "$\delta\iota\delta\acute{\alpha}\sigma\kappa\omega$," *TDNT* 5, 153ff.

[13]See M. Hengel, *The Charismatic Leader and His Followers* (trans. J. Greig; New York: Crossroad, 1981) 42ff.; M. Smith, "A Comparison of Early Christian and Early Rabbinic Tradition,'" *JBL* 82 (1963) 169-176; and W.D. Davies, "Reflections on a Scandinavian Approach to 'the Gospel Tradition,'" in *Neotestamentica et Patristica, Freundsgabe Oscar Cullmann* (NovTSup 6; Leiden: Brill, 1962) 14-34.

[14]See Hengel, *Charismatic Leader*, 42ff.

[15]See Davies, "Reflections."

memorize his words. It should also be noted that the function of the rabbinic pupil was to study Torah. As will be seen below when we examine the missionary charge to the Twelve (6:7-13), Jesus' disciples are not called to study Torah but to engage in an active missionary enterprise in which they preach repentance, cast out demons, and heal the sick.

Jesus was not a rabbi. Although he argued with opponents, Jesus' method is hardly in the rabbinic tradition. In fact, he usually argues exegetically (e.g., by interpreting Old Testament words or passages) only when asked or challenged by a third party. He uses parables and proverbs not to explain and clarify Torah, but to set forth his own eschatological[16] message. Jesus should be seen, therefore, as outside the discoverable teaching traditions of Judaism.[17]

Although Jesus himself was not recognized as a Zealot leader, the fact that Simon "the Zealot" was numbered among the apostles (Lk. 6:15; Acts 1:13) leads some to conclude that "the profession of Zealot principles and aims was not incompatible with intimate participation in the mission of Jesus."[18] What follows from this not widely accepted conclusion is the suggestion that the relationship between the political, military revolutionary leader and his followers provides a good model to explain Christian discipleship. The one called was expected to leave possessions and family and join the charismatic leader in battle against the Romans. Usually the revolutionary leader demanded total allegiance to his person.

This model of discipleship is closer to Jesus' discipleship than the rabbinic example, but it too fails at important points. Jesus does not put himself at the head of a guerilla band. The notion of "holy war" seems foreign to him as he prefers to talk of war against demonic powers and of his powerful word as the only weapon. In addition, "zealousness" is played down in

---

[16]From the Greek for "end," 'ἐσχατον. Eschatology is literally the teaching about the last things (e.g., the end of the world, judgment) or the final age.

[17]Hengel, *Charismatic Leader,* 49. See also Donaldson, "Called,'" 67-69.

[18]S.G.F. Brandon, *Jesus and the Zealots* (New York: Scribner's, 1967) 355.

the Synoptics (Matthew, Mark, and Luke). According to Luke 9:51f., for example, Jesus' disciples wanted to act like Zealots and call down fire from heaven against those who opposed their master. Jesus does not agree with this and sternly rebukes them.[19]

Unlike the Zealots, Jesus devoted himself to the whole people, not just a select group of followers. He did call individuals to follow him, but he continued to remain open to all. This is apparent when one considers that the tax collector Levi was numbered among the special companions of Jesus.

The best master/disciple model for our purposes is found in the Old Testament relationship between Elijah and Elisha. Elisha is faithful to Elijah from beginning to end. According to 1 Kings 19:19-21, Elijah finds Elisha busy plowing. He casts his mantle on Elisha as a sign of his call and immediately Elisha follows him. Elisha then asks for and receives permission to say goodbye to his parents. Once he returns, Elisha remains faithful to Elijah until the later's ascension.

Like Elisha, the disciples of Jesus leave everything to follow their master. Other similarities are seen most clearly in Luke's account of Jesus' ministry. In Luke 9:61f., an intensification of the call of Elisha, Jesus does not allow his disciple to bid farewell to those at home. Jesus' call here is patterned after Elijah's, but Jesus is seen to demand more. Once the call to follow has been accepted, Jesus' disciples, like Elisha, remain faithful to their master until his ascension. Just like Elisha, the followers of Jesus must put their fate and future into the hands of the master.[20]

In spite of these similarities, one must understand that there is an important difference between the call to follow Jesus and the Elijah-Elisha narrative. In every Old Testament call narrative the one who calls is ultimately God, whether a prophet is charged with issuing the call or God personally summons an individual by means of a vision. Jesus' call to

[19]See J.M. Ford, *My Enemy Is My Guest* (Maryknoll: Orbis, 1984), whose thesis is that Luke presents Jesus as an advocate of nonviolence, forgiveness, and practical love of enemies.

[20]See P. Hinnebusch, *Jesus, The New Elijah* (Ann Arbor: Servant, 1978).

discipleship, on the other hand, occurs by virtue of his own messianic authority.[21] This allows us to conclude that Jesus is not calling his disciples in exactly the same way as Elijah called Elisha. In spite of these differences, however, the Elijah-Elisha relationship remains as the most appropriate Jewish model for understanding Jesus' call to discipleship.

As we mentioned above, in Mark 1:16-20 it is Jesus who takes the initiative and calls the first disciples to follow him and to become "fishers of men." In order to do this, to follow Jesus literally, these individuals had to leave their homes, their occupations, and their relatives. While the basic act of discipleship is to follow Jesus, the consequences of this choice are total commitment to this new way of life and commitment to an unknown and uncertain future. The verb $\mathring{\alpha}\kappa o\lambda o\upsilon\theta\varepsilon\hat{\imath}\nu$ (to follow) can be understood literally, as "to accompany, go after, or go along with a person in time and place," or metaphorically or religiously, as "to follow someone as that person's disciple."[22] In many instances Mark clearly uses this verb to indicate entry into special communion with Jesus (2:14, 15; 8:34; 9:38; 10:21, 28).[23] Used in this sense it is synonymous with discipleship. In other instances Mark seems to intend that $\mathring{\alpha}\kappa o\lambda o\upsilon\theta\varepsilon\hat{\imath}\nu$ be understood in a literal way.[24]

What does Mark want us to understand about "following Jesus" in 1:16-20? At first glance it seems that these verses are meant to be read literally; the four fishermen left their homes, occupations, and relatives to travel with Jesus. But when Jesus promises that in the future they will be "fishers of men" he introduces a missionary element into the call. Above all, then, this is a call to service. Jesus has invited these fishermen to assist him in drawing individuals "out of the waters of this world into the eschatological life of the age to come."[25]

---

[21] Hengel, *Charismatic Leader,* 67ff.

[22] BAGD, 31.

[23] Perhaps 10:32, 52 and 15:41 should be read this way also.

[24] 3:7; 5:24; 6:1; 11:19; 14:13, 54. See G. Kittel, "'$\alpha\kappa o\lambda o\upsilon\theta\acute{\epsilon}\omega$," *TDNT* 1, 213f.

[25] D.E. Nineham, *Saint Mark* (Pelican Gospel Commentaries; Baltimore: Penguin, 1963) 71.

That "following Jesus" involves service of one kind or another is seen throughout the Gospel. Mark tells us that Jesus himself "came not to be served but to serve (διακονεῖν) (10:45). Especially interesting in this regard is the fact that the women who witnessed the crucifixion are said to have "followed ('ακολουθεῖν) him and ministered (διακονεῖν) to him" (15:41). Although they are never called disciples, perhaps Mark wants his readers to understand that these women, who "followed" and "ministered" to Jesus, are in fact disciples.[26] If this is Mark's intent then he would agree with Luke, who presents the mother of Jesus and other women as model disciples, individuals who "hear the word of God and do it" (Lk. 8:21).[27]

Regardless of how one reads 15:41, it is clear that the call to follow Jesus in Mark 1:16-20 is not simply an invitation to walk alongside Jesus.[28] The element of service involved indicates that 'ακολουθεῖν is being used here in the narrower sense of a commitment which breaks all previous ties.

The Call of Levi (2:13-17)

[13]He went out again beside the sea; and all the crowd gathered about him, and he taught them. [14]And as he passed on, he saw Levi the son of Alphaeus sitting at the

---

[26]*Contra* R.P. Meye *Jesus and the Twelve: Discipleship and Revelation in Mark's Gospel* (Grand Rapids: Eerdmans, 1968) 121-122; and P.S. Pudussery, "The Meaning of Discipleship in the Gospel of Mark," *Jeevadhara* 10 (1980) 100. See G. Lohfink, *Jesus and Community* (trans. J.P. Galvin; New York: Paulist; Philadelphia: Fortress, 1982) 91-92; W. Munro, "Women Disciples in Mark?" *CBQ* 44 (1982) 225-241; M.J. Selvidge, "'And Those Who Followed Feared' (Mark 10:32)," *CBQ* 45 (1983) 396-400; and E. Schüssler Fiorenza, *In Memory of Her* (New York: Crossroad, 1983) 316-323.

[27]See e.g., R.F. O'Toole, *The Unity of Luke's Theology* (Wilmington: Michael Glazier, 1984) 118-126 and C.H. Talbert, *Reading Luke* (New York: Crossroad, 1984) 90-94.

[28]See 5:18-20 where the Gerasene who has just been healed does not literally follow Jesus but does in fact do what the Twelve have been called to do, preach/proclaim (3:14).

tax office, and he said to him, "Follow me." And he rose
and followed him.

[15]And as he sat at table in his house, many tax collectors
and sinners were sitting with Jesus and his disciples; for
there were many who followed him. [16]And the scribes of the
Pharisees, when they saw that he was eating with sinners
and tax collectors, said to his disciples, "Why does he eat
with tax collectors and sinners?" [17]And when Jesus heard it,
he said to them, "Those who are well have no need of a
physician, but those who are sick; I came not to call the
righteous, but sinners."

Mark integrates the call of Levi, son of Alphaeus (2:14),
into a series of controversy dialogues (2:1–3:6) by connecting
it with 2:15-17. In its present location it serves as an
introduction to the narrative concerning Jesus' table fellowship with tax collectors and sinners (2:15-17). It is reasonable
to conclude that Mark inserted this story here in order to
make a point about the kind of individuals who followed
Jesus as his disciples. Jesus not only eats with tax collectors
and sinners; he also calls them to be his followers.

As has been alluded to above, this call story shares many
similarities with the call of the first disciples in 1:16-20.
(1) Jesus issues the invitation to Levi. (2) The call was issued
by Jesus "as he passed on" (2:14). (3) Jesus calls the son of
Alphaeus from his place of work. (4) The tax collector is
summoned to an exclusive attachment to the person of Jesus.
(5) Levi responds immediately. (6) In order to obey Jesus and
follow him, Levi must break ties with his tax office.[29]

The initiative has once again come from Jesus. Levi is
pictured as sitting at his tax office, apparently engaged in
tasks which comprised his normal daily activities as a tax
collector. There is no indication that this son of Alphaeus had
ever set eyes on Jesus before the moment recorded in Mark

[29]Although Levi is given no specific commission by Jesus, E. Best, *Following
Jesus: Discipleship in the Gospel of Mark* (JSNTSup 4; Sheffield: JSOT, 1981) 178,
suggests that by inviting those who need the gospel to his house where the gospel is
proclaimed (2:17), Levi has become a "fisher of men."

2:14. He receives this gratuitous invitation not just to "follow," to leave his own way, but to "Follow me," to form a personal attachment to Jesus and join Jesus on his way. The next words in the text, "And he rose and followed him," suggest that Mark wants the reader to understand that Levi responded to Jesus' invitation/command immediately, as did the first disciples (1:18, 20). Levi's obedient response to the call of Jesus also appears to have resulted in his leaving his tax office, just as the first disciples separated themselves from their occupation when Jesus summoned them to follow him.

It is also significant that, in this passage (2:13-17), Mark is expanding the circle of disciples to include "sinners" explicitly for the first time. Jesus' call to sinners should be seen as a call to discipleship, which will result in repentance and faith, and not just a call to repentance (cf. Lk. 5:32).[30] In the same way that Jesus came to call ($\kappa\alpha\lambda\epsilon\hat{\imath}\nu$) James and John (1:19-20) to follow him, so too he came to call ($\kappa\alpha\lambda\epsilon\hat{\imath}\nu$) sinners.[31] This is supported by: (1) the suggestion that Levi, who is called to attach himself to the person of Jesus, is a sinner,[32] and (2) the fact that the following two pericopes focus on Jesus' defense of his disciples against charges that they are sinners, i.e., that they do not fast (2:18-22) and that they break the law (2:23-28).

The Selection of The Twelve (3:13-19)

> [13]And he went up into the hills, and called to him those whom he desired; and they came to him. [14]And he appointed twelve, to be with him, and to be sent out to

[30]E. Schweizer, *The Good News According To Mark* (trans. D.H. Madvig; Richmond: John Knox, 1970) 65-66.

[31]Mark uses $\kappa\alpha\lambda\hat{\epsilon}\imath\nu$ four times in his Gospel. In addition to these two calls to discipleship (1:20; 2:17), the term appears when Jesus' family "calls" him (3:31), and when Jesus asks (11:17), "Is it not written, 'My house shall be called a house of prayer for all nations?'" (Isa. 56:7).

[32]Best, *Following,* 177, and P.J. Achtemeier, *Invitation to Mark* (Garden City: Doubleday, 1978) 50-51.

preach [15]and have authority to cast out demons: [16]Simon whom he surnamed Peter; [17]James the son of Zebedee and John the brother of James, whom he surnamed Boanerges, that is, sons of thunder; [18]Andrew, and Philip, and Bartholomew, and Matthew, and Thomas, and James the son of Alphaeus, and Thaddaeus, and Simon the Cananaean, [19]and Judas Iscariot, who betrayed him.

Mark summarizes the first major part of his Gospel in 3:7-12, which also serves as a transition to the second part.[33] Once again, one notes that Mark has singled out discipleship as an important theme, for this section also begins with the call of disciples. The same elements seen in the earlier call stories (1:16-20; 2:13-17) are also found here. (1) It is Jesus who calls. (2) This call requires the kind of obedience that entails forsaking old ties. (3) The call that Jesus issues is one that involves service.

Jesus calls whom he desires and they come to him. Again the gratuitous nature of the call is emphasized, as there is no reason given for the selection of these specific individuals. They are not presented as holier than others. The only thing that distinguishes them from others is that Jesus has called them. When Jesus called the first disciples, they responded immediately (1:18; cf. 1:20). One gets a similar impression as Mark closely connects Jesus' invitation, "Follow me," with the report that Levi "rose and followed him" (2:14). This time, in 3:13, the immediacy of the response is captured by the phrase "and they came to him," which follows directly after we are told that Jesus "called to him those whom he desired."

The demand for radical obedience and exclusive attachment to the person of Jesus seems to be represented in this call story by the comment that Jesus appointed twelve "to be with him" (3:14), while the missionary element, "to be fishers of men" (1:17), is expanded as "to be sent out to preach and have authority to cast out demons" (3:14-15).

Those who respond to the call of Jesus are required to

---

[33]Schweizer, "Portrayal," 388 and Perrin, *The New Testament,* 245.

attach themselves both to the person and to the work of Jesus. They must follow him/be with him and be "fishers of men"/preach and cast out demons. Mark never really says explicitly what "being with Jesus" means; rather he shows us throughout his Gospel.

At the very least "being with" Jesus involves seeing his works and hearing his words.[34] The disciples remain constantly at Jesus' side except when he separates from them to pray (1:35; 6:46; 14:32, 35, 39), when the Twelve are sent on a special mission (6:13-30), and when they abandon him (14:50).[35] After the resurrection the disciples are to be reunited with Jesus (16:7) who is still leading the way (14:28). In addition to this physical understanding of "being with" Jesus there also seems to be an interior attachment of fidelity. The call to become a companion of Jesus, an associate in ministry, suggests something more than mere physical presence.[36]

According to Mark, "being with" Jesus is a necessary preparation for being sent out by Jesus.[37] There can be no doubt that those sent out are commissioned to do the things that Jesus does. Mark introduces Jesus to us in his first chapter as one who preaches and casts out demons (1:39), teaches (1:21-22), and heals the sick (1:32-34). In chapter six of Mark we learn that those Jesus has chosen to send out, preach (6:12), teach (6:30), and heal the sick and cast out demons (6:13). Disciples of Jesus must be committed to his person and his mission.[38]

---

[34]Meye, *Jesus and the Twelve,* 103.

[35]See B. Rigaux, *The Testimony of St. Mark* (Chicago: Franciscan Herald, 1966) who lists fourteen passages in Mark that refer to the disciples being with Jesus. Matthew and Luke, in their parallel accounts, omit reference to the disciples and speak only about Jesus. This highlights Mark's interest in this aspect of discipleship.

[36]See K. Stock, *Boten aus dem Mit-Ihm-Sein: Das Verhältnis zwischen Jesus und den Zwölf nach Markus* (AnBib 70; Rome: Biblical Institute, 1975), who argues that "being with Jesus" is the most important feature of discipleship in Mark's Gospel.

[37]M.F. Kirby, "Mark's Prerequisite For Being An Apostle." *TBT* 18 (1980) 77-81.

[38]D. Catchpole, "Discipleship, The Law, and Jesus of Nazareth," *Crux* 11 (1973) 8, states that "there never has been Christianity without mission."

This call to close communion with Jesus obviously involves
the formation of a new community made up of those who
follow Jesus (10:28) and now constitute the real family of
Jesus (3:20-35). While this will be discussed further below, it is
important to note here that recognition of the significance of
this communal aspect of discipleship has led many to
conclude that "it is only in community that genuine discipleship can be carried out . . . . Isolated discipleship simply does
not exist in the Gospel of Mark."[39]

The importance of community, "being with" Jesus, and
doing the things of Jesus is summarized nicely in Kelber's
claim that, "What lies at the root of the Markan gospel is
therefore the desire to remain in living attachment to Jesus
and to preserve continuity between Jesus and the Markan
community of followers."[40]

The Missionary Charge to the Twelve (6:7-13)

[7]And he called to him the Twelve, and began to send
them out two by two, and gave them authority over the
unclean spirits. [8]He charged them to take nothing for their
journey except a staff; no bread, no bag, no money in their
belts; [9]but to wear sandals and not put on two tunics. [10]And
he said to them, "Where you enter a house, stay there until
you leave the place. [11]And if any place will not receive you
and they refuse to hear you, when you leave, shake off the
dust that is on your feet for a testimony against them." [12]So
they went out and preached that people should repent.
[13]And they cast out many demons, and anointed with oil
many that were sick and healed them.

Because Mark relates not only the choosing of the Twelve
but also their actual sending out, it would be wise for us to
examine at this point the pericope in which Jesus issues his

[39]H.F. Peacock, "Discipleship in the Gospel of Mark," *RevExp* 75 (1978) 563.
[40]*Kingdom,* 5.

missionary charge to the Twelve (6:7-13). The twelve disciples who were called (1) to "be with" Jesus and (2) to join him in his ministry are now sent out as missionaries. The close relationship between these two pericopes is obvious to readers of Mark's Gospel. The author has even used the same verbs, προσκαλεῖσθαι (to call), and 'αποστέλλειν (to send), in both passages.

After Jesus calls these disciples to him, he gives them "authority over the unclean spirits" (6:7) and sends them out in pairs to preach and exorcise. This is what we were told would happen in 3:14-15. The obedience of these disciples is apparent as we soon discover that they did exactly as they had been told: "So they went out and preached that people should repent. And they cast out many demons, and anointed with oil many that were sick and healed them" (6:12-13).

These missionaries left everything behind as Jesus "charged them to take nothing for their journey except a staff" (6:8). This call for confidence, courage, and perseverance (they will not always be successful, cf. 6:10) reminds us of the initial call of Jesus for repentance (found here in 6:12) and faith (1:15). The disciples are being reminded to trust and be dependent on God and not to seek security in themselves.

Genuine discipleship, therefore, has a missionary dimension. It is not simply an interior spiritual quest. Those who were called to "be with" Jesus were also sent into the world to preach, exorcise, and heal. Once again we learn that Christian discipleship is dynamic and not static.

The Call of the Rich Man (10:17-22)

[17]And as he was setting out on his journey, a man ran up and knelt before him, and asked him, "Good Teacher, what must I do to inherit eternal life?" [18]And Jesus said to him, "Why do you call me good? No one is good but God alone. [19]You know the commandments: 'Do not kill, Do not commit adultery, Do not steal, Do not bear false witness, Do not defraud, Honor your father and mother.'" [20]And he

said to him, "Teacher, all these I have observed from my youth." [21]And Jesus looking upon him loved him, and said to him, "You lack one thing; go, sell what you have, and give to the poor, and you will have treasure in heaven; and come, follow me." [22]At that saying his countenance fell, and he went way sorrowful; for he had great possessions.

Most who examine the call stories in Mark's Gospel limit their comments to the passages already discussed. There is, however, one more pericope in which Jesus explicitly calls an individual to follow him. Unlike our previous examples, in this instance the invitation of Jesus is refused.

The story of the Rich Man (10:17-22) has many similarities with those call stories examined above. (1) Jesus issues the invitation (2) to form an exclusive relationship with himself. (3) The call was issued as Jesus was journeying. (4) In order to follow Jesus this individual would have had to leave behind all that he had.

The first verse of this story tells us that the encounter between Jesus and the rich man (In spite of the traditional name for this passage there is no indication in Mark that he was young) took place as Jesus was "setting out on his journey" (10:17). This is reminiscent of Jesus' call of the first disciples as he was "passing along by the Sea of Galilee" (1:16) and the call of Levi "as he passed on" (2:16). Jesus is pictured as someone who is on the move and following Jesus involves joining him on his journey.

The call to "Follow me" is issued by Jesus in 10:21 just as it was in 1:17 and 2:14. In fact, the same words used to call this individual, 'ακολούθει μοι (Follow me), were used to call Levi. We saw earlier that a positive response to Jesus' invitation resulted in the separation from one's relatives and occupation. It was obvious in the previous call stories that there was a "cost" to discipleship, but Jesus never explicitly stated what this "cost" would be. In this pericope the cost is made painfully clear. The rich man is told to sell what he has, give to the poor, and then follow Jesus (10:21).

This is actually a rather tragic story. An individual both

desired to fulfill and actually fulfilled the commandments, yet he realized that more was necessary for salvation than merely following the rules. Jesus agreed with his conclusion and informed the man that he could attain his goal of eternal life only if he would sell what he had, give to the poor, and "follow me." But it was this that the rich man could not bring himself to do.

Although this call to separate oneself from earthly possessions is common to most of the call stories we have discussed, one should be careful before insisting that this is an absolute requirement of Christian discipleship. Jesus has consistently invited people to form a personal relationship with himself, not with a set of old or new rules and regulations. The command to sell all and give to the poor is not meant to be seen as just one more rule which everyone must follow. As far as we can tell, Jesus himself did not always require that everything be sold and the proceeds given to the poor (cf. 14:3-9). And although the literal following of the earthly Jesus seems to have been very important, Jesus did not always insist that his supporters leave everything in order to follow him (cf. 5:18-19).

What we have seen thus far is that the appropriate response of every individual called by Jesus must involve absolute obedience and total devotion to God. Would-be followers of Jesus must rid themselves of anything and everything that prevents them from taking Jesus and his call seriously. The obstacle which stood in the way of the individual in this pericope was his wealth. At this time, in this place, the vast possessions of this rich man prevented him from committing himself completely to Jesus.

The fact that this command is specifically addressed only to this one individual, however, should not blind us to Jesus' overwhelmingly negative attitude toward riches. A person's wealth can easily stand in the way of total obedience to God; it can give the individual a false sense of security and independence. Riches can also lead to the oppression and exploitation of the poor and defenseless. Jesus probably issued these warnings about the dangers of wealth and vast possessions because in Palestinian society riches had already become a widely recognized source of alienation from God and oppression of the poor.

Although we have been concentrating on the failure of the rich man to accept Jesus' invitation to follow him, we must not ignore the fact that there is a very close connection between the story of the rich man (10:17-22) and the verses which follow (10:23-31).

> 23And Jesus looked around and said to his disciples, "How hard it will be for those who have riches to enter the Kingdom of God!" 24And the disciples were amazed at his words. But Jesus said to them again, "Children, how hard it is to enter the Kingdom of God! 25It is easier for a camel to go through the eye of a needle than for a rich person to enter the Kingdom of God." 26And they were exceedingly astonished, and said to him, "Then who can be saved?" 27Jesus looked at them and said, "With human beings it is impossible, but not with God; for all things are possible with God." 28Peter began to say to him, "Lo, we have left everything and followed you." 29Jesus said, "Truly, I say to you, there is no one who has left house or brothers or sisters or mother or father or children or lands, for my sake and for the gospel, 30who will not receive a hundredfold now in this time, houses and brothers and sisters and mothers and children and lands, with persecutions, and in the age to come eternal life. 31But many that are first will be last, and the last first."

The theme of possessions as an obstacle to following Jesus becomes a general warning that riches are a hindrance to those who wish to enter the Kingdom of God. The disciples react to this statement with amazement. After commenting in general about how difficult it is for anyone to enter the Kingdom of God, Jesus again turns his attention to the rich and states that their entry into the Kingdom is virtually impossible. The disciples are shocked and openly wonder if salvation is possible for anyone. Jesus calms their fears and reminds them of the power of God. Salvation is possible, but the way of discipleship is very difficult.

After hearing the exchange between Jesus and the rich man, as well as Jesus' additional words, Peter reminds Jesus of how costly following him has already been for himself and the other disciples. They have abandoned everything in order to follow Jesus (10:28). Mark's careful use of the words ’αφιέναι (to leave) and ’ακολουθεῖν (to follow) should remind us of the call of the first disciples (1:16-20).[41] Jesus answers Peter by admitting the difficulty of discipleship, and adding that in spite of the hardship involved, faithful following will result in joy both in this life and in the age to come (10:29-30).

The requirements of discipleship mentioned here by Jesus are ones we have seen before. The would-be follower of Jesus must renounce totally and absolutely all previous relationships and all possessions. The focus has shifted, however, from the rich man who was unable to commit himself completely to Jesus because of his possessions to the difficulties any disciple might face in seeking to enter the Kingdom of God. The "many possessions" (10:22) of the rich man have become house, brothers, sisters, mother, father, children, and lands (10:29). No longer is the discussion about almsgiving; now the focus is on the requirement for radical renunciation and separation from all that stands in the way of total commitment to the person of Jesus.

This rather peculiar promise, that the followers of Jesus will receive compensation in the present, and not just "in the age to come," for what they have left behind is best understood as referring to the formation of a new eschatological community. We will examine this communal dimension of Christian discipleship below.

Because the rich man was unable to separate himself from his many possessions, the little band that followed Jesus was one fewer than it might have been. The important point being made here should not escape us; Jesus' call to discipleship can be refused. There is a choice involved.

That the call of God demands a freely given response on the

[41]*Ibid.*, 89.

part of the one called is also seen in several important stories contained in the Hebrew Scriptures. The Lord tells Moses (Ex. 19:5) to inform the children of Israel that they shall be his own possession among all peoples *if* they will obey his voice and remain faithful to the covenant (a solemn, almost legal bond between God and the people of Israel). Yahweh invites the people to enter an ongoing covenant relationship that would require strict obedience to covenant legislation. Moses reports this offer of the Lord to the people who freely respond, "All that the Lord has spoken we will do" (Ex. 19:8). After the descendants of these Israelites enter the Promised Land, Joshua gathers them together at Shechem and recites the history of God's dealings with the chosen people from the call of Abraham until the recent conquest of Canaan. At the end of this recitation Joshua suggests that the people "serve the Lord." He adds, however, "if you be unwilling to serve the Lord, choose this day whom you will serve . . . but as for me and my house, we will serve the Lord" (Josh. 24:14-15). In spite of the fact that they freely chose to follow the Lord, we soon learn that many of the Israelites who settled into the land of Canaan "have forsaken the commandments of the Lord and followed the Baals" (1 Kgs. 18:18). Yahwism and Baalism (the worship of the fertility god of Canaan) have become so intertwined that the Israelites stand in puzzled silence when the prophet Elijah gives them a choice: "If Yahweh is God, follow him; but if Baal, then follow him" (1 Kgs. 18:21).

The call of the Lord is compelling, but it does not overpower a person to the extent that free choice is an impossibility. The Israelites at Mt. Sinai, Shechem, and Mt. Carmel were free to respond positively or negatively to the call of God communicated to them by Moses, Joshua, and Elijah. Because of the story of the rich man we now know that the powerful authoritative call of Jesus can also be refused.

Conclusion

Those who are included among the disciples of Jesus are individuals who have been called by him. More often than not this invitation comes during the normal course of their daily activities. Those chosen to receive this call to follow Jesus appear to have been rather ordinary individuals. They are not called to study Torah, but issued an invitation to enter into an intimate relationship with Jesus himself.

These would-be disciples must "repent and believe in the gospel" (1:15). What is involved here is a radical conversion. They must abandon their old way of life and totally commit themselves to the person and work of Jesus. Nothing must stand in the way of their exclusive relationship with Jesus, neither possessions, nor occupations, nor relatives.

The call to "be with" Jesus is also a call to service. The faithful follower is one who shares in and continues the preaching, teaching, and healing ministry of Jesus. Genuine discipleship, therefore, is not merely an interior spiritual quest; it is active and not static. The disciple of Jesus is called to serve other members of the eschatological community (cf. 1:31) and, through the missionary enterprise, those outside the faith community as well.

2

Where Does One Find Mark's Teaching on Discipleship?

Our inclusion of the call of Levi, the commissioning of the Twelve, the missionary charge to the Twelve, and the story of the rich man (obviously not one of the Twelve, even potentially) among the calls to discipleship raises the question, "Where does one find Mark's teaching on discipleship?" The answer is that Mark's teaching on discipleship is found throughout the Gospel, in passages dealing explicitly with the Twelve, but also in pericopes in which disciples, those who "follow" Jesus, and those who do not follow him appear. In order to demonstrate this we will have to examine pericopes involving a number of individuals and groups in Mark's Gospel. We will begin by discussing the relationship between the Twelve and the disciples, since there is some question about whether or not Mark understands the Twelve as identical to the disciples.

Are "the Disciples" and "the Twelve" Identical?

Those who respond positively to the call of Jesus and who follow him are usually referred to by Mark either as "the

Twelve" (*οἱ δώδεκα*) (10 times)[1] or "the disciples" (*οἱ μαθηταί*) (41 times).[2] Scholarly opinion runs the gamut from those who believe that in Mark's Gospel "the disciples" and "the Twelve" are interchangeable terms,[3] to those who argue that in Mark "the term 'disciple' is never limited to the Twelve. . . or identified exclusively with them."[4] Most scholars avoid both extremes and conclude that the terms are frequently, but not always, interchangeable.[5]

As the Gospel now stands, it is highly unlikely that Mark intends his readers to understand that every time he says "the disciples" he really means the Twelve. We first hear of Jesus' "disciples" in the call of Levi (2:15-16). Mark tells us that "many tax collectors and sinners were sitting with Jesus and his disciples," when the Pharisees asked "his disciples" why Jesus ate with these kinds of people. Prior to the call of Levi only four individuals, Peter, Andrew, James, and John, had responded to Jesus' invitation to follow him. Therefore, it is unlikely that in this case "the disciples" refers to the Twelve. We also read about "his disciples" plucking grain on the sabbath (2:23), withdrawing with Jesus to the sea (3:7), and receiving instructions from Jesus to ready a boat for his use (3:9) before we are told that Jesus ascends the mountain and chooses twelve "to be with him, and to be sent out to preach and have authority to cast out demons" (3:14). The readers of Mark's story about Jesus encounter his "disciples" five times before being told that a group of twelve has been formed.

[1] Without the article in 3:14, but with the article in 4:10; 6:7; 9:35; 10:32; 11:11; 14:10, 17, 20, 43.

[2] Frequently with one of the following possessives: Jesus', his, your, my. In all cases Jesus' disciples are clearly distinguished from the disciples of John and the disciples of the Pharisees.

[3] C.H. Turner, "Marcan Usages VIII: The Disciples and the Twelve," *JTS* 28 (1926-27) 22-30; See also, Meye, *Jesus and the Twelve,* e.g., 137 173, 210 and S. Freyne, *The Twelve: Disciples and Apostles* (London: Sheed and Ward, 1968) 110ff.

[4] Peacock, "Discipleship in the Gospel of Mark," 556.

[5] See e.g., E. Best, "Mark's Use of the Twelve," *ZNW* 69 (1978) 35 and "The Role of the Disciples in Mark," *NTS* 23 (1976/77) 380-381. Cf. H. Fleddermann, "The Discipleship Discourse (Mark 9:33-50)," *CBQ* 43 (1981) 59.

Apparently, Mark does not think he is referring to the Twelve when, in these instances, he uses the term "his disciples."

It is possible, of course, that the disciples referred to in these passages are only those who will be included later (3:14ff.) among the Twelve. There are serious arguments against this, however. (1) According to most scholars, the call of Levi (2:13-14) is the call of a disciple. Therefore it seems that, according to Mark, an individual could become a disciple of Christ without being listed among the Twelve.[6] (2) Further evidence that discipleship is not limited to the Twelve in Mark's view is seen in 2:16 where we read that "many tax collectors and sinners were sitting with Jesus and his disciples; for there were many who followed him." Most commentators understand this last clause to be referring to the number of disciples who followed Jesus.[7] (3) In 3:13ff., we read that Jesus "went up on the mountain, and called to him those whom he desired; and they came to him. And he appointed twelve, to be with him, and to be sent out to preach and have authority to cast out demons." The opinion of the vast majority is that Jesus has singled out twelve from a larger number of disciples who have just been called.[8] Prior to 3:14, therefore, Mark does not use "the disciples" and "the Twelve" as interchangeable terms; there is a wider group of disciples than twelve.

After the Twelve are called, however, we see that there are many similarities between them and the disciples. It has been pointed out that the disciples, who are passing through Galilee with Jesus and hear his second passion prediction, are

---

[6]P.J. Achtemeier, "'And He Followed Him': Miracles and Discipleship in Mark 10:46-52," *Semeia* 11 (1978) 115-145, and Best, "Mark's Use of the Twelve," 32.

[7]Nineham, *Saint Mark,* 100; Best, "Mark's Use of the Twelve," 32; and V. Taylor, *The Gospel According to St. Mark* (2nd ed.; London: Macmillan, 1966) 205. For an opposing view see Freyne, *The Twelve,* 110f. and Meye, *Jesus and the Twelve,* 140ff.

[8]Nineham, *Saint Mark,* 116; Best, "Mark's Use of the Twelve," 32; and Taylor, *St. Mark,* 230, who states that "The Twelve are not identical with 'the disciples,' nor with 'the Apostles,' who represent a circle wider than that of the Twelve." For an opposing view see Freyne, *The Twelve,* 107ff. and Meye, *Jesus and the Twelve,* 146ff.

to be identified with the Twelve whom Jesus teaches in 9:35ff.[9]
After entering Jerusalem and looking around at everything,
Jesus goes out to Bethany "with the Twelve" (11:11). On the
following day when they come from Bethany, it is mentioned
that "his disciples" (11:14) heard Jesus curse the fig tree. In
14:12ff. we read:

> [12]And on the first day of Unleavened Bread, when they
> sacrificed the passover lamb, his disciples said to him,
> "Where will you have us go and prepare for you to eat the
> passover?" [13]And he sent two of his disciples, and said to
> them, "Go into the city, and a man carrying a jar of water
> will meet you; follow him, [14]and wherever he enters, say to
> the householder, 'The Teacher says, Where is my guest
> room, where I am to eat the passover with my disciples?'
> [15]And he will show you a large upper room furnished and
> ready; there prepare for us." [16]And the disciples set out and
> went to the city, and found it as he had told them; and they
> prepared the passover.
> [17]And when it was evening he came with the Twelve.
> [18]And as they were at table eating, Jesus said, "Truly, I say
> to you, one of you will betray me, one who is eating with
> me."

It is "his disciples" who ask Jesus, "Where will you have us go
and prepare for you to eat the passover?" (14:12), and
"disciples" (14:13,14,16) he sends out to find the proper place.
But it was with "the Twelve" that Jesus came to the upper
room.[10]
   This does not mean that one should equate the disciples
and the Twelve on every occasion after the formation of the
latter group. For example, in 3:31-35 we see Jesus inside a
house with a crowd seated "around him ($\pi\epsilon\rho\grave{\imath}\ \alpha\upsilon'\tau\acute{o}\nu$)" This is

[9]Fleddermann, "Discipleship Discourse," 59. See also Best, "Mark's Use of the
Twelve," 21, who concludes with respect to 9:35 that Mark's "editorial work serves
to turn the emphasis from the twelve to a less determinate body, the disciples."

[10]Once this is recognized, different conclusions are still possible. See Freyne, *The
Twelve,* 109, and Best, "Mark's Use of the Twelve," 30.

the position usually taken by disciples who are listening to their teacher. In contrast, his mother and brothers are standing "outside" asking for Jesus to come "outside." When he is informed that his family is calling for him, Jesus responds, "Who are my mother and my brothers?" Jesus answers his own question when he identifies "those who sat about him (τοὺς περὶ α'υτόν) as his true family: "And looking around on those who sat about him, he said, 'Here are my mother and my brothers! Whoever does the will of God is my brother, and sister, and mother' " (3:34-35). In the next pericope we find Jesus teaching beside the sea. After addressing a huge crowd (4:1ff.), he begins a series of private instructions to "those who were about him (οἱ περὶ αυ'τόν) with the Twelve" (4:10). At the end of this secret instruction we read that "privately to his own disciples (μαθηταί) he explained everything" (4:34).

> **3** 31And his mother and his brothers came; and standing outside they sent to him and called him. 32And a crowd was sitting about him; and they said to him, "Your mother and your brothers are outside, asking for you." 33And he replied, "Who are my mother and my brothers?" 34And looking around on those who sat about him, he said, "Here are my mother and my brothers! 35Whoever does the will of God is my brother, and sister, and mother."

> **4** Again he began to teach beside the sea. And a very large crowd gathered about him, so that he got into a boat and sat in it on the sea; and the whole crowd was beside the sea on the land. 2And he taught them many things in parables . . . ."

> 10And when he was alone, those who were about him with the Twelve asked him concerning the parables.

> 33With many such parables he spoke the word to them, as they were able to hear it; 34he did not speak to them without a parable, but privately to his own disciples he explained everything.

It is reasonable to assume that "those who were about him (τοὺς περὶ αὐτόν)" in the house (3:32, 34), those identified by Jesus as his true family, are the same as "those who were about him (οἱ περὶ αυ 'τόν) with the Twelve" (4:10), those identified at the end of the discourse as "disciples" (4:34). It seems clear, therefore, that in this pericope the Twelve are associated with a larger group of believers.[11]

On the way to Jerusalem (10:32), as Jesus is about to deliver his third passion prediction, we read: "And they were on the road, going up to Jerusalem, and Jesus was walking ahead of them; and they were amazed, and those who followed were afraid. And taking the Twelve again, he began to tell them what was to happen to him." The first group of Jesus' traveling companions, identified in this verse as on the road walking behind Jesus, can only be "the disciples" mentioned in the previous pericope (10:23, 24). A second, potentially different group walking behind Jesus are "those who followed."[12] "The Twelve" represent the third potentially different group mentioned as being with Jesus. It appears, therefore, that on at least these two important occasions (4:10 and 10:32) Mark has distinguished between "the Twelve" and a larger group of disciples.[13] Thus the only possible conclusion is that Mark does not use "the disciples" and "the Twelve" as interchangeable terms in the sense that whenever the disciples are mentioned the reader is expected to understand this as referring to the Twelve. It is clear that for Mark "disciple" can ⚡ refer to a wider group than the Twelve.

[11]Kelber, *Kingdom*, 26, 31, and Best, "Mark's Use of the Twelve," 16-18. See also, R.C. Tannehill, "The Disciples in Mark: The Function of a Narrative Role," *JR* 57 (1977) 388 n.8, and J.R. Donahue, *The Theology and Setting of Discipleship in Mark* (Milwaukee: Marquette University, 1983) 32-37. For a contrary view see Meye, *Jesus and the Twelve*, 148-152, and Freyne, *The Twelve*, 111f.

[12]See Taylor, *Mark*, 437, and those he lists as supporting this position, Swete, Lagrange, Gould, Plummer, RV, RSV, and Moffatt. For an opposing view see Meye, *Jesus and the Twelve*, 159-164.

[13]Donahue, *Discipleship in Mark*, 8, and Best, "Mark's Use of the Twelve," 21-24, who notes that Mark's composition of verse 32 "shows that he wishes to widen what was said to the twelve so that it becomes relevant for all disciples, i.e., all his community."

What is the Role of the Twelve?

Can the Twelve be expanded to represent any and all disciples? Or, is there some task or function that pertains only to the Twelve? As one looks more closely at Mark's Gospel, it is clear that there are really four different groups of people that follow Jesus: an inner core of three or four, the Twelve, the disciples, and a larger group that followed Jesus and/or participated in his ministry. Peter, James, and John (and sometimes Andrew) form this special inner group that is given new names (3:16-17), witness the raising of Jairus' daughter (5:37), are present at the Transfiguration (9:2-9), ask Jesus privately the question which leads to his second major speech in Mark (13:3-37), and go off with Jesus while he prays in Gethsemane (14:32ff.).

In Mark's Gospel this intimate group of three or four individuals joins together with others to form a group known as the Twelve. It is this group, the Twelve, who are formally appointed (3:14-15) to be with Jesus and "to be sent out to preach (κηρύσσειν) and have authority to cast out demons." Although neither "the disciples" nor the members of the larger group that followed Jesus and/or participated in his ministry are specifically appointed to be "with" Jesus, they are, in fact, present with him on numerous occasions during his ministry. The intimate relationship suggested when Jesus calls the Twelve to be "with him" appears to be possible for all when Jesus says, "Whoever does the will of God is my brother, and sister, and mother" (3:35). Thus, while it is important to be "with" Jesus, it is not clear that the Twelve are "with" Jesus in a different sense from "the disciples" or the others who followed him are "with" Jesus.[14]

In addition to being appointed to be "with" Jesus, the Twelve were given "authority to cast out demons." But those referred to as Jesus' "disciples" are also pictured as attempting

---

[14]Best, "Mark's Use of the Twelve," 34. See Stock, *Boten,* 177, 185, who argues that Mark uses the Twelve to suggest that discipleship involves a theological progression from the initial stage of being called to growth in one's personal relationship with Jesus.

to exorcise during his ministry (9:14-29). It is true, of course, that the disciples are unsuccessful in their attempt to cure the possessed boy. But this is meant to highlight the importance of faith, prayer, and the power of God operative in Jesus, not to suggest that the disciples are unsuccessful, and the Twelve successful, exorcists. The appropriateness of this conclusion is obvious when one looks at the story of the Strange Exorcist which appears later in Chapter 9. In 9:38 one of the inner circle, John, tells Jesus that he and the others forbade a man from "casting out demons ... because he was not following us." Jesus displays an extremely open and tolerant attitude as he responds, "Do not forbid him; for no one who does a mighty work in my name will be able soon after to speak evil of me" (9:39). It is possible, therefore, for one who is not a follower of Jesus to be doing the work specifically assigned to the Twelve (3:14-15).[15]

The Twelve, who were appointed to be "with" Jesus and to "have authority to cast out demons," were also "to be sent out to preach." At first glance it seems significant that while the Twelve are to have a preaching ministry, those referred to as Jesus' "disciples" in Mark are not portrayed as preaching. It has been pointed out on numerous occasions, however, that others, not part of the Twelve, not even explicitly called "disciples," participate in this role.[16] The healed leper (1:45) went out to talk freely and spread ($\kappa\eta\rho\acute{u}\sigma\sigma\epsilon\iota\nu$) the news. After crossing the sea to the country of the Gerasenes, Jesus healed the demoniac who "began to proclaim ($\kappa\eta\rho\acute{u}\sigma\sigma\epsilon\iota\nu$) in the Decapolis how much Jesus had done for him" (5:20). Witnesses to the healing of the deaf mute also proclaimed ($\acute{\epsilon}\kappa\acute{\eta}\rho\upsilon\sigma\sigma\text{o}\nu$) the marvelous thing that Jesus had done (7:36f.). Once again we see that something which appears at

[15]See Fleddermann, "Discipleship Discourse," 66, who argues that Mark portrays the strange exorcist as one who "serves."

[16]J. Dewey, *Disciples of the Way: Mark on Discipleship* (Cincinnati: Women's Division, Board of Global Ministries, The United Methodist Church, 1976) 50; J.R. Donahue, "A Neglected Factor In The Theology of Mark," *JBL* 101 (1982) 582-585 and *Discipleship in Mark,* 9; Schweizer, "Portrayal," 172-173; and Tannehill, "Narrative Role," 404.

first to be exclusive to the Twelve in the final analysis can be said as well of others in Mark's Gospel.

It is important to note, however, that in most cases the preaching/ proclaiming of those not included among the Twelve seems to be presented as problematic, something that interferes with Jesus' functioning freely and contradicting his explicit command (1:44-45; 7:36). Since the content of the preaching of the Twelve is said to be "repentance" (6:12), perhaps wonder-working for its own sake, and not repentance, would have been emphasized in the preaching/ proclaiming of the leper and the witnesses to the healing of the deaf mute. Any emphasis on Jesus only as a miracle worker is opposed to Mark's message of suffering Messiahship as we will see below in chapter 3.

We have already discussed how future members of the Twelve (1:16-20) and Levi (2:14) "followed" Jesus. But there are also others mentioned in the Gospel, never explicitly referred to as "disciples" or members of the Twelve, who "follow" Jesus on his way to the cross. The blind beggar Bartimaeus, after he receives his sight, "follows" Jesus on the way (10:52).[17] And the women who witnessed the crucifixion are said to have "followed" Jesus when he was in Galilee (15:40-41). Thus we are led to the same conclusion: people not referred to specifically as "disciples" or members of the Twelve do what the closest associates of Jesus do.

The women are an especially interesting group since they are the only individuals who specifically obey Jesus' command to "be servants of all." The only time Mark uses the noun διάκονος (servant) is in the discipleship discourses following the second and third passion-resurrection predictions (9:35; 10:43). The corresponding verb, διακονεῖν (to serve), is used only four times in the Gospel. At the end of the temptation scene, angels serve/wait on Jesus (1:13). In a mid-section passage which will be examined below Jesus says that he came "to serve," not to be served (10:45). Elsewhere in Mark it is only women who obey this command of Jesus. Peter's

---

[17]Achtemeier, "'And He Followed,'" argues that this is a story about discipleship.

mother-in-law "serves" Jesus and his companions (1:31) and the women who had followed Jesus had also served him (15:41). Although never called "disciples," these women did what the disciples and the Twelve were called to do as they both "followed" Jesus and "served" him.

It is obvious from the foregoing that most of the functions mentioned in 3:14-15 are not restricted to the Twelve. Is there anything that pertains only to the Twelve? The answer to this question depends on how one answers several other questions. (1) Is Mark exclusively interested in presenting a negative portrait of the Twelve? (2) Are the references to the Twelve traditional or redactional? (3) Does Mark present a clear development of other early Christian views of the Twelve?

Some scholars conclude that Mark is interested in presenting a consistently negative picture of the Twelve.[18] They claim that Mark is writing against individuals within his own community who hold an erroneous Christology or an erroneous eschatology. The Twelve, then, are said to function primarily as representatives of those Mark is combating. For reasons that will be explained more thoroughly below, we join with most scholars and conclude that Mark presents a complex picture of "the disciples" and is not interested only in focusing on their darker side. Therefore, in Mark's Gospel the Twelve do not function exclusively as representatives of a heretical position within the Markan community.

The majority response to the second question also deserves our allegiance. There are many redactional references to the Twelve in Mark, but there are also a number of references which are traditional.[19] In writing his Gospel, Mark used traditional material, material that had been passed on by the earliest Christian communities both orally and in pre-Gospel written collections. The assumption of modern scholarship is that Mark also redacted (i.e., collected, arranged, and edited) what he received in order to produce the final document, his Gospel, as a deliberately organized whole. It is the task of the

---

[18]See our more detailed analysis in chapter 4 below.

[19]See Best, "Mark's Use of the Twelve."

interpreter to determine the nature and extent of the author's activity "in collecting and creating, as well as in arranging, editing, and composing."[20] Such an examiniation leads most scholars to conclude that the oral and/or written tradition which Mark received already contained references to the Twelve.

The answer to the third question is that Mark does not present a clear development of other early Christian views of the Twelve. Inquiries into the origin of "the Twelve" in the Christian tradition usually focus either on Matthew 19:28 (Lk. 22:30) or on 1 Corinthians 15:5. The first theory traces the origin of the Twelve to the preaching ministry of the historical Jesus. In the only saying about the purpose of the Twelve attributed to Jesus himself, we learn that he chose them to sit on (twelve) thrones judging the twelve tribes of Israel (Mt. 19:28; Lk. 22:30). The language is that of traditional apocalyptic,[21] and appears to refer to the final coming of the Kingdom of God. It also suggests that the Twelve are the eschatological nucleus of the new people of God, and heirs to the twelve tribes of Israel. Just as the twelve sons of Jacob/Israel were present at the beginnings of the original Israel, so the Twelve are present at the beginning of the renewed Israel. The second theory traces the origin of the Twelve to the post-resurrection community. Paul's mention of the appearance of the risen Christ to Peter and to the Twelve (1 Cor. 15:5) suggests to some that "the Twelve" were the creation of the early Christian community which saw the resurrection of Jesus as the beginning of the new age and the recipients of a resurrection appearance as the nucleus of a new community.[22]

---

[20]N. Perrin, *What is Redaction Criticism?* (Philadelphia: Fortress, 1969) 2.

[21]From the Greek word for "revelation or disclosure," ' $\alpha\pi o\kappa\acute{\alpha}\lambda\upsilon\psi\iota\varsigma$. Apocalyptic literature claims to derive from heavenly visions and usually offers a view of the future which is consoling to those who suffer for doing the will of God.

[22]For a summary of these positions see Donahue, *Discipleship,* 6-7; and G. Schmahl, *Die Zwölf im Markusevangelium: Eine redaktionsgeschichtliche Untersuchung* (TTS 30; Trier: Paulinus, 1974) 1-15; Cf. also Best, "Mark's Use of the Twelve," 30, 35.

Both these early Christian views of the Twelve focus on the "twelve tribe" symbolism of Israel and see these intimate followers of Jesus as the eschatalogical nucleus of the new people of God. Mark appears to know that twelve is a symbolic number for the tribes of Israel,[23] but he does not develop this in such a way that the Twelve are presented as the "eschatological nucleus of a new community."[24]

> In that very place where one would expect a saying like Lk. 22:29-30, that is, in response to the request of John and James to sit at the right and left hand of Jesus in his glory (10:37), there is no mention that they will judge twelve tribes. Also Mark has no resurrection appearance to the twelve and even in that verse which is viewed by many scholars as a promise of such an appearance, the charge of the messenger is "go tell his disciples and Peter," *not* "the twelve and Peter."[25]

What then is Mark's particular theological understanding of the Twelve? First, the Twelve are included in Mark's Gospel because this term was present in the tradition used by Mark.[26] After a careful analysis of the texts in which the Twelve appear, Ernest Best concludes that the tradition portrayed: (1) the Twelve as recipients of special teaching (4:10; 9:35; 10:32; cf. 10:41), and (2) Judas as a member of the Twelve.[27] In addition, (3) the reference to the missionary commission in 3:14 probably was attached to the Twelve in the pre-Markan tradition.[28] Second, Mark's redactional use of the Twelve[29]

[23]The inclusion of the number twelve in 3:14 suggests this. See also our comments in chapter 6 below.

[24]Best, "Mark's Use of the Twelve," 30, 35.

[25]Donahue, *Discipleship,* 7.

[26]*Pace* R. Bultmann, *History of the Synoptic Tradition* (3rd ed. trans. J. Marsh; New York: Harper & Row, 1963) 345.

[27]At least one of the references to the betrayer Judas as a member of the Twelve is widely recognized as traditional (14:10, 20, 43).

[28]"Mark's Use of the Twelve," 13-15, 32. Best also includes 6:43 and 11:11 as probably pre-Markan.

[29]*Pace* Meye, *Jesus and the Twelve.*

serves (1) to blur any distinction between them and the disciples and (2) to emphasize the missionary dimension of discipleship. There is a basic similarity between the Twelve and the disciples (i.e., service, especially within the community) and a possible distinction (i.e., active missionary work).

Mark intentionally blurs the distinction between the Twelve and the disciples because he is not interested in setting up an inner "college," an eschatological nucleus, or in having the Twelve seen only as a group from the past with no relevance for his readers. Although he does not omit the term when it is present in the tradition, Mark regularly introduces "the disciples" in places where we might expect him to introduce "the Twelve," if the latter was his favorite term. He has taken the traditional picture of the Twelve as recipients of Jesus' special instruction and added numerous redactional passages in which special instruction is given to disciples (4:34; 9:31; 10:10; 11:14). On at least two occasions he shows Jesus instructing simultaneously the Twelve and a larger group (4:10; 10:32).[30] Mark does not demote the Twelve, but rather turns them into representatives of every Christian disciple. He is more interested in this symbolic role of the Twelve than in their historical role as the intimate companions of Jesus. Mark wants his readers to understand that the Twelve are disciples and that the lessons taught to the Twelve are not restricted to them. In this way Mark intends his teaching on discipleship to apply to his own community and not be limited to a story about the past. What is taught to the Twelve is meant for all disciples, all the church, to hear.[31]

Scholars have recognized that there is a strong missionary dimension in many of the narratives in which the Twelve appear.[32] The common theme of 3:14 and 6:7, for example, is the sending out of the Twelve. This emphasis on activity to be conducted among those outside the community gathered

[30]Best, "Mark's Use of the Twelve," 34.

[31]*Ibid.,* 26.

[32]R. Pesch, *Das Markusevangelium* (2 vols.; HTKNT 2; Freiburg/Basel/Wien: Herder, 1976-77) I, 205, and Best, "Mark's Use of the Twelve," 15, 33ff., and *Following,* 183-185.

around Jesus has led to the suggestion that Mark uses the Twelve to represent those who are engaged in active missionary work. While the association of the Twelve with the missionary reference in 3:14 is probably traditional, the reference to their missionary activity in 6:7-13 is very likely redactional.[33] In other words, Mark emphasizes the role of the Twelve as missionaries, which he found in the tradition, by his editorial activity in composing the missionary charge to the Twelve (6:7ff.). If there is anything unique to the Twelve in Mark, therefore, it is this missionary activity.

Although "disciples" are never formally commissioned as missionaries, they are, at times, given what might be considered missionary responsibilities toward those outside the community: "Peter and Andrew are called to be 'fishers of men' (1:17); exorcism is not restricted to the Twelve (9:29; 38f.); care for the more material needs of others is implied in 9:36f. and 10:21f.; 14:28 and 16:7 probably represent Mark's general commission to the church to be active in mission work."[34]

Conclusion

Where does one find Mark's teaching on discipleship? Frequently the person who is interested in "discipleship" answers this question by focusing exclusively on those passages in which individuals referred to as "disciples" appear. Occasionally one also finds readers assuming that Mark is using "the disciples" and the Twelve" as interchangeable terms. Our investigation of this last assumption led to the conclusion that these terms are frequently, but not always, interchangeable. For Mark, therefore, "disciple" can refer to a wider group than the Twelve. This conclusion caused us to ask whether or not there was some task or

---

[33]Best, "Mark's Use of the Twelve," 13-16.

[34]*Ibid.,* 33. See also T.E. Boomershine, "Mark 16:8 and the Apostolic Commission," *JBL* 100 (1981) 225, 238.

function that pertained only to the Twelve. In examinig the role of the Twelve in Mark's Gospel we discovered that virtually everything which appears to be exclusive to the Twelve can be said as well of others. If there is anything unique to the Twelve in Mark it is their activity as missionaries.

That discipleship is not limited to the Twelve or the historical disciples or followers of Jesus is clear also from those texts containing universal moral directives. Readers of Mark's Gospel surely are meant to see themselves addressed when Jesus says: "Whoever would be great among you must be your servant, and whoever would be first among you must be slave of all" (10:43-44); "If anyone would come after me, let that person deny him/herself and take up his/her cross and follow me" (8:34); and "It is easier for a camel to go through the eye of a needle than for a rich person to enter the Kingdom of God" (10:25).[35]

Mark's teaching on discipleship, therefore, is found throughout the Gospel, in passages dealing explicitly with the Twelve, but also in pericopes in which disciples, those who "follow" Jesus, and those who do not follow him appear. As we continue our examination of Christian discipleship according to Mark, we will have to be attentive to what Mark says throughout the Gospel and not limit our investigation only to those passages which deal explicitly with the Twelve or those called disciples.

[35]Q. Quesnell, *The Mind of Mark* (Rome: Pontifical Biblical Institute, 1969) 134-138.

3

The Central Section of Mark's Gospel

The Central Section of Mark's Gospel (8:22–10:52) appears to be the most carefully crafted unit of the entire Gospel.[1] It is set off from the rest of the Gospel by two stories in which Jesus restores someone's sight—the blind man at Bethsaida (8:22-26) and blind Bartimaeus (10:46-52). These two pericopes represent the only times in Mark's Gospel when Jesus gives sight to those who are physically blind. The compositional technique being employed here, "intercalation," is characteristic of this Gospel writer. Frequently Mark uses framing stories or framing verses to help the reader interpret the intervening section. Well-known examples of this technique are the fig tree story (11:12-14 and 11:20-26) which brackets the cleansing of the Temple (11:15-17), and the comments about Jesus' "teaching" (1:12-22 and 1:27) which surround his first exorcism (1:23-26). Mark wants his readers to understand that what Jesus did at the beginning and end of his journey—open the eyes of the blind—he also attempted to do while he was traveling along the way from Caesarea Philippi to Jerusalem. Between these stories of how Jesus cured the physical blindness of the man from Bethsaida (8:22-26)

---

[1]Perrin, *The New Testament*, 248, and Kelber, *Kingdom*, 67.

and Bartimaeus (10:46-52)[2] we find him attempting to cure the spiritual blindness of the disciples. This is clear not only from Mark's "sandwich technique," but also from the fact that 8:22-26 follows the discussion about the multiplication stories in 8:14 -21, including the reference to Jeremiah 5:21 ("Hear this, O foolish and senseless people, who have eyes, but see not, who have ears, but hear not") and Ezekiel 12:2 ("Son of man, you dwell in the midst of a rebellious house, who have eyes to see, but see not, who have ears to hear, but hear not"; cf. Mk. 8:18). Throughout this entire central section of the Gospel Jesus is pictured as opening the eyes of his disciples to a new dimension of his messiahship.[3] These intimate companions of Jesus must "see" (i.e., understand) the necessity of his suffering and death and what significance these have for the correct understanding and practice of discipleship.

The superstructure on which this entire midsection seems to rest is the motif of the "way."[4] By means of geographical references and journey notices, reminders that Jesus and his followers are traveling, Mark emphasizes the fact that discipleship is active and not passive, that it means leaving one's own way to follow Jesus on his way. This theme is also present in the call stories, but it is more fully developed here in the central section of the Gospel.

As the journey begins, Jesus and his disciples are reported to be "on the way" (8:27) toward Caesarea Philippi, to the north of Galilee. The central secton ends in the south as Jesus and his disciples are leaving Jericho for Jerusalem and Bartimaeus is said to have followed Jesus "on the way"

---

[2]There may be some significance to the fact that Jesus sends the first man home, while Bartimaeus follows him. Perhaps Bartimaeus is allowed to follow because he recognizes that Jesus is the son of David. Since the first individual demonstrates no knowledge of Jesus' identity, he could only have presented Jesus to others as a miracle worker. The emphasis on Jesus exclusively as a miracle worker is opposed to Mark's message of suffering Messiahship. For a different explanation of how the Bartimaeus story fits into Mark's understanding of discipleship, see Achtemeier, " 'And He Followed.' "

[3]Bultmann, *HST*, 350.

[4]Kelber, *Kingdom*, 67ff.

(10:52). The "way" motif is not limited to these verses, however; it is emphasized at various points throughout the journey. Not long after the trip begins we learn that Jesus and his followers have moved from Caesarea Philippi to Galilee (9:30), specifically to Capernaum (9:33). At this point in the midsection we discover that the disciples have engaged in conversations "on the way" (9:33-34). The little band continues its journey southward as Mark reports that Jesus went to Judea and beyond the Jordan (10:1). Then, while he is traveling "along the way" (10:17), Jesus engages in a discussion with a rich man (examined above) about what must be done to inherit eternal life (10:17-22). Both the movement of Jesus and the goal of the journey are clearly marked in 10:32 where we learn that Jesus and hs disciples are "on the way, going up to Jerusalem."

By means of these frequently recurring references to the way, Mark presents Jesus' life as a journey. His careful use of geographical references shows the reader that Jesus is not aimlessly wandering around the countryside; Jesus' journey has a specific goal and purpose. As he goes from Caesarea Philippi to Jerusalem with his disciples, Jesus reveals to them his identity, the goal of his journey, and what being his follower entails.

Although the motif of the "way" is seen most clearly in the central section of the Gospel, it is not limited to these verses. We have already seen that Jesus invites his first disciples to follow him as he is "passing along by the Sea of Galilee" (1:16). The call of Levi took place as Jesus "passed on" (2:14) and the discussion with the rich man (part of the central section, but examined above) occurs as Jesus is "setting out on his journey" (10:17). Thus, we have already learned that discipleship is dynamic and consists of following Jesus "on the way." Those who accept Jesus' invitation to be "with" him must join him as he travels "on the way" toward his goal.

It is entirely possible that Mark wants his readers to view Jesus' whole life as a journey. In the first few verses of the Gospel we learn that John the Baptist prepares the "way" of

Jesus.[5] Mark may have joined together Isaiah 40:3 ("A voice cries: 'In the wilderness prepare the way of the Lord, make straight in the desert a highway for our God.' ") and Malachi 3:1 (" 'Behold, I send my messenger to prepare the way before me...' ") because both reference the "way," a theme Mark wanted to introduce early and to which he refers throughout the Gospel.[6] There might also be special significance in the fact that Mark pictures Jesus as "walking ahead" of his disciples "on the way to Jerusalem" (10:32). Jesus does more than just preach the way; he literally shows the way. And Jesus will continue to lead the way, to "go before" his disciples, even after his death and resurrection (14:28; 16:7) .

The central section of Mark's Gospel, which concerns us now, is further subdivided by the three passion-resurrection predictions. Each of these predictions takes place in a different location and follows almost immediately after the geographical locaton is mentioned. Shortly after we learn that Jesus and his disciples are at Caesarea Philippi (8:27) we encounter the first passion-resurrection prediction (8:31-33). The second and third predictions are reported immediately after we are told that Jesus and his band are passing through Galilee (9:30) and are "on the way" to Jerusalem (10:32)

Readers who discover this pattern of geographical reference followed by passion-resurrection prediction usually note that there are additional similarities among these three accounts. Each time Jesus predicts his passion and resurrection, one or more disciples misunderstand his teaching. After the first passion-resurrection prediction (8:31), Peter refuses to accept the necessity of Jesus' suffering and death and rebukes Jesus; he, in turn, is rebuked by Jesus (8:32-33). The disciples do not understand (9:32) the second passion-resurrection prediction (9:31) and are so self-centered that they have been discussing "with one another who was the greatest" (9:33-34). After the third prediction (10:33-34), we see James and John, the sons

[5]The programmatic nature of the "way" motif in 1:2-3 was seen by A. M. Ambrozic, *The Hidden Kingdom* (CBQMS 2; Washington, D.C.: The Catholic Biblical Association of America, 1972) 19-20.

[6]Kelber, *Kingdom*, 67 n. 2.

of Zebedee, asking for positions of special honor for themselves. They too have failed to understand the real meaning of the coming death and resurrection of Jesus.

Confronted with the failure of disciples to "see" (i.e., understand), Jesus teaches his followers what discipleship entails. A discourse on discipleship is located immediately after each of the misunderstanding passages. They represent the fourth and final part of the fixed pattern apparent here in the central section of the Gospel. It is these passages (8:34–9:1; 9:35-37; 10:42-45) that will be examined more closely below.

As Jesus moves from north to south, his identity, his purpose, and the requirements of discipleship should become clearer both to the disciples and to the readers of the Gospel. All would-be followers of Jesus face a crisis as each must answer the question Jesus asks his original disciples, "Who do you say that I am?" (8:29). And how one answers this crucial queston makes all the difference in the world. Insight into the nature and destiny of Jesus leads to a better understanding of one's own nature and destiny. The disciples in Mark struggle with this new revelation about the suffering, death, and resurrection of Jesus. They have a difficult time understanding who Jesus is and what following him really requires. The reader of the first half of the Gospel, although in a better position than the Markan disciples, may have similar problems. What we must do now is journey with Jesus from Ceasarea Philippi to Jerusalem, examine the three discipleship discourses he delivers along the way, and allow our eyes to be opened to this new dimension of discipleship. What, then, do these passages add to our understanding of the requirements of discipleship?

The First Discipleship Discourse (8:34–9:1)

Immediately following the healing of the blind man at Bethsaida (8:22-26), we learn that Jesus and his disciples are on the way to Caesarea Philippi (8:27). As they are traveling, Jesus asks them what others say concerning his identity. After they respond, he poses a similar question to them, "Who do you say that I am?" (8:29). Peter takes the initiative and answers that Jesus is "the Christ." As readers of Mark's Gospel, we soon learn that this confession can only be correct if Peter understands "Christ" to mean the Son of Man who must suffer and die. Jesus tells us this in his first passion-resurrection prediction (8:31-33). That Peter does not understand "Christ" in this way is clear from his reaction to Jesus' claim that the passion-resurrection is a divine necessity. Perhaps Peter should be seen as representing the general Jewish expectation at the time of Jesus, that the Messiah would be a political king and military leader who would drive out the Romans.[7] Whatever Peter's concept of messiahship is, it is not the same as Jesus' concept.

With this misunderstanding, the first three parts of the pattern, the naming of the geographical location, the prediction of the passion-resurrection, and the misunderstanding of a disciple, have been completed. What remains is Jesus' discipleship discourse.

> **8** [34]And he called to him the multitude with his disciples, and said to them, "If anyone would come after me, let that person deny him/herself and take up his/her cross and follow me. [35]For whoever would save his/her life will lose it; and whoever loses his/her life for my sake and the gospel's will save it. [36]For what does it profit a person, to gain the whole world and forfeit his/her life? [37]For what can a person give in return for his/her life? [38]For whoever is ashamed of me and of my words in this adulterous and sinful generation, of that person will the Son of Man also be ashamed, when he comes in the glory of his Father with the holy angels." **9** [1]And he said to them, "Truly, I say to you, there are some standing here who will not taste death before they see the Kingdom of God come with power."

[7]See e.g., G. Vermes, *Jesus the Jew* (New York: Macmillan, 1973) 129-156.

There is virtual unanimity among scholars that the passion of Jesus dominates 8:27ff. as Mark presents his "theology of the cross." This section, 8:34 –9:1, and the two other mid-secton discipleship discourses are the places where the way of Jesus to the cross and the way of discipleship are most clearly interwoven. Jesus does not explain why it is necessary that the Christ, the Son of Man, suffer and die, but he does say that all who wish to follow him must be willing to give up their lives.

The similarity between the destiny of Jesus and that of his disciples is seen clearly in these verses, just as it was in the call and commissioning stories. After speaking of his own impending suffering, death, and resurrection (8:31), Jesus states that anyone who would follow him also must be ready to suffer and die. At the same time he promises final salvation to those who take up their cross and follow him (9:1).[8] The ultimate goal of following Jesus, therefore, is to share in the glory of the coming Son of Man and the joys of the Kingdom of God (9:1, 47; 10:15, 23, 24, 25).

Jesus addresses the multitude as well as his disciples when he states that anyone who wants to come after him must take up his/her cross and follow him. In these verses, the cost of discipleship is presented before Jesus issues his command/ invitation to "Follow me" (8:34). This was also the case in the story of the rich man (10:17-22), examined above. A major difference between these two passages, however, is the universal applicability of the demand in 8:34. Addressed as it is to everyone, disciples and potential disciples, the demand to take up your cross and follow Jesus represents a significant addition to our previous understanding of the requirements of discipleship.

It is widely accepted that Mark understands Jesus' words on cross-bearing to apply to discipleship in his own day. Therefore, before any commitment to follow Jesus is made, every potential disciple should understand exactly what the cost of discipleship includes. What, then, does denying

---

[8]So Ambrozic, *Hidden Kingdom*, 235, who says, "To the Christian reader of the Gospel Mk. 9:1 thus gives the assurance of glory after humiliation and suffering." See also Best, *Following Jesus,* 44.

oneself and taking up one's cross actually entail?

Since the death of Jesus was mentioned only a few verses earlier (8:31), this demand to take up one's cross is best seen as referring to Jesus' own death.[9] Mark's initial intent, then, is to present Jesus as anticipating his own violent death in Jerusalem and insisting that others be ready to share that end. The saying in 8:35 seems to confirm this: "For whoever would save his/her life will lose it; and whoever loses his/her life for my sake and the gospel's will save it."

It is generally assumed that Mark wrote his Gospel in and for a community which was suffering persecution, and in some cases death, for the sake of Christianity. In such a situation, those who desired to save their lives (8:35a) could often do so by renouncing their faith in Christ. The benefits of such apostasy would be a longer life and increased material prosperity. At the final judgment, however, the verdict will go badly for those who choose to behave in this manner. This should remind us of the rich man who chooses the enjoyment of his possessions in the present over the possibility of eternal life (10:17-22).

The second half of the verse (8:35b) provides a contrast with the first and tells the reader that those who willingly accept loss, suffering, and death for the sake of Christ and his gospel will receive a favorable verdict in the coming judgment. Jesus delivers a similar message to his followers in the pericope which contrasts the disciples and the rich man (10:23-31). In those verses, Jesus tells Peter and the others that anyone who has left home, family and possessions "for my sake and the gospel" will receive, among other things, "persecutions, and in the age to come eternal life" (10:29-30).

At the very least, then, we can conclude that this verse about taking up one's cross, as it now stands in Mark's Gospel, refers to the death of Jesus (explicit in 8:31). In its present location it also informs the original disciples that they might have to lose their lives for the sake of Jesus and the

[9]D.R. Fletcher, "Condemned to Die," *Int* 18 (1964) 156-164. See also J. G. Griffiths, "The Disciple's Cross," *NTS* 16 (1970) 358-364.

gospel (8:35). And, because Mark understands this verse to have universal application (as was mentioned above), it also applies to later followers of Jesus who will suffer martyrdom. The initial readers of Mark's Gospel would have been familiar with this especially cruel form of capital punishment known as crucifixion. Death by crucifixion for crimes, such as robbery or some form of resistance to Roman imperialism, was a familiar site in Galilee under Roman rule.[10] In most cases people condemned to be crucified were ordered to carry their own crosses, or at least the crossbar, to the place of death.[11] For Mark's readers, then, these words on cross-bearing surely would have evoked "the picture of a condemned man going out to die."[12]

There is a problem here, of course, and caution must be exercised in explaining what is meant by taking up one's cross. If cross-bearing is taken too literally, then this particular demand of discipleship is irrelevant to the life of most disciples. Since there is no indication that Mark expected all future disciples would have to undergo martyrdom, it is appropriate to ask in what sense this command could be a universally binding condition of discipleship.

While an overly literal explanation of this verse is to be avoided, the solution is not to be found in jumping to the opposite extreme. Some readers have concluded that the cross to which Jesus refers is best understood as patient endurance of whatever trials, sorrows, or disappointments one may meet. Those who adopt this position should be very cautious, as they run the risk of diluting the message of Mark. We must remember, after all, that Jesus is talking about his

[10]While the debate about Mark's original audience continues, it is safe to say that our conclusion would be the same regardless of whether Mark wrote his Gospel to the Christian community in Galilee [cf. Kelber, *Kingdom*, 129ff.] or in Rome [cf. M. Hengel, "The Gospel of Mark: Time of Origin and Situation," in *Studies in the Gospel of Mark* (trans. J. Bowden; Philadelphia: Fortress, 1985) 1-30].

[11]P. Parker, "Crucifixion," *IDB* 1, 747.

[12]Fletcher, "Condemned," 163, accepts this saying as genuine. While this is debated in scholarly circles, there is general agreement that regardless of whether or not the logion is original, Mark's readers would have understood these verses in the way suggested above.

own impending death on the cross, not the normal bumps and
bruises of daily life.

Most helpful in solving our problem is the suggestion that
what this verse urges is the "denial of self." [13] This must not be
confused with the commonly understood meaning of self-
denial, to abstain from certain luxuries. Jesus is not talking
about the denial of things to the self. He is speaking about the
denial of "the self," making oneself not an end but a means.
The follower of Jesus must be willing to make any sacrifice,
even life itself, for Christ. Anyone who wants to follow Jesus
must be prepared to suffer the same fate that he suffered.
Discipleship means following Jesus in the way of the cross,
which includes a readiness for martyrdom (8:34).[14]

Disciples and readers alike now know that Jesus' messiahship includes suffering and death. It is also clear that the
disciple who wants to share in the glory of the Son of Man at
his coming must be willing to suffer the same fate. While this
ultimate sacrifice will not be required of all, the life of every
disciple must be characterized by the denial of self, the living
of a nonegocentric existence. This message seems to anticipate
the theme of the second and third midsection discipleship
discourses, servanthood. In 9:35 Jesus says, "If anyone would
be first, that person must be last of all and servant of all."
And, in 10:45 Jesus speaks of servanthood and the cross when
he says that "the Son of Man also came not to be served but to
serve, and to give his life as a ransom for many."

One can conclude, then, that in these verses which comprise
the first midsection discipleship discourse, Mark tells us that
followers of Jesus must value Jesus and the gospel more than
their own lives. Disciples are not to be preoccupied with
themselves and the amassing of possessions (8:36). Just as
Jesus makes a deliberate choice to do God's will (14:36) so

[13]Best, *Following*, 37, and H. E. Luccock, "The Gospel According to St. Mark,"
IB, 7, 770.

[14]V. K. Robbins, "Summons and Outline in Mark: The Three-Step Progression,"
NovT 23 (1981) 108, says that the central principle of discipleship is "that he who
wishes to save his life must accept a form of discipleship in which he is willing to
lose his life."

would-be disciples must make a deliberate choice to take up their cross and follow Jesus. This decision for or against Jesus and his other-directed way of life is not to be viewed lightly, because one's eternal destiny hangs in the balance. Jesus warns those who refuse to follow him on his way through suffering and death that they can only expect negative consequences for themselves when the Kingdom of God comes in its fullness (8:38).

A word of consolation immediately follows and serves to balance off this rather ominous warning (8:38). Jesus assures those who refuse to be ashamed of either him or his words that they will be rewarded at the parousia for their faith and perseverance (9:1). In the future, when the Kingdom of God comes in its fullness, those who have taken up their cross and followed Jesus will be members of this Kingdom.[15]

The Second Discipleship Discourse (9:35-37)

Jesus and his disciples are soon on the move southward, toward Jerusalem. As they are passing through Galilee (9:30) Jesus delivers his second passion-resurrection prediction (9:31). The pattern, outlined above, is continued here as once again we learn that misunderstanding follows Jesus' announcement of his impending death and resurrection (9:32). The total incomprehension of the disciples, to all that Jesus has taught thus far about his fate and what it means to follow him, is seen in their dispute about which one is the greatest. On the way to Jesus' death in Jerusalem we find the disciples talking about personal advancement. Their concern for their personal prestige, their own ranking among the Twelve, shows how far they are from true discipleship which calls for the renunciation of one's own ego and the willingness

---

[15]It is generally accepted that Mark 9:1 presents Jesus as expecting the Kingdom of God to arrive in its fullness in the very near future. If this means that Jesus did not know the exact day or hour of the parousia, it is no more than Mark portrays Jesus as admitting in 13:32. Regardless of the timetable, the decision to take up one's cross and follow Jesus continues to have eternal consequences.

to follow Jesus even to the point of losing one's life.

The disciples in Mark's Gospel continue to have a difficult time understanding what it means to follow Jesus. What does Jesus' second midsection discipleship discourse add to our understanding of the demands of discipleship?

> **9** [35]And he sat down and called the Twelve; and he said to them, "If anyone would be first, that person must be last of all and servant of all." [36]And he took a child, and put him in the midst of them; and taking him in his arms, he said to them, [37]"Whoever receives one such child in my name receives me; and whoever receives me, receives not me but him who sent me."

Some insist that the way of the cross is Mark's theme here, in the second discipleship discourse, just as it clearly was in 8:34–9:1.[16] While the second passion prediction does see Jesus' impending death as the goal of the path he is following, explicit references to the cross (as found in 8:34–9:1) are missing from this discipleship discourse (9:35-37). Jesus says here that the one who would be first must be servant of all (vs. 35). It is possible, of course, to define servant in terms of 9:31 and Jesus' death for all. But it is also possible that service is meant to be understood in a broader sense.[17] Just as carrying one's cross was seen as involving more than being crucified as Jesus was, so too service should be seen as not limited only to dying for others.

What then does it mean to be a "servant ($\delta\iota\acute{\alpha}\kappa o\nu o\varsigma$) of all"? The Markan Jesus illustrates what he means in verses 36-37 when he places a child in the midst of his disciples and says, "Whoever receives one such child in my name receives me; and whoever receives me, receives not me but him who sent me" (vs. 37). In Matthew's parallel version of this story (Mt. 18:1-5) the child serves as an example for the disciples to copy.

---

[16]See e.g., P. J. Achtemeier, "An Exposition of Mark 9:30-37," *Int* 30 (1976) 178-183.

[17]See Fleddermann, "Discipleship Discourse," 57-75, and Dewey, *Disciples of The Way*, 81ff.

Some commentators have argued that it is also Mark's intent to portray the child in 9:36-37 as a model of the Christian.[18] Usually mentioned are: (1) The fact that only a few verses later, Jesus warns that it would be better for a person to be thrown into the sea with a millstone for a necklace than to cause one of "these little ones" who believe in him to sin (9:42). If the "little ones" referred to in this verse are meant to be understood as followers of Jesus, and if the "child" of 9:36-37 is to be identified with the "little ones" of 9:42, then it is possible to argue that the child is meant to be seen as a model of the Christian disciple. (2) The similarity between 9:36-37 and 10:13-16 where, it is claimed, the child serves as a model for the disciples of Jesus. This approach leads to the conclusion that humility and lowliness ought to be characteristic of the followers of Jesus.

The problem, however, is that the servant in 9:36-37 is not the child, but the one who "receives" the child in Jesus' name. Mark does not focus on the attitude of the child, but on the attitude of others toward the child. To "receive" a child in this context seems to mean to take care of or show kindness to. It suggests the kind of service that would be rendered to a guest, in this case a guest sent by God.[19] A child in the Greco-Roman world of Jesus and Mark was considered unimportant and had no status in the eyes of the world. But it is just such a person who must be the object of concern for the followers of Jesus. Serving all, including the powerless and helpless, is serving Jesus and his Father. Just as disciples are called to lose their lives for the sake of Jesus (8:34-9:1) so are they called to serve for his sake. Jesus served by literally giving his life for others. We must follow his example by seeing ourselves as last and least, not insisting on our own prerogatives but always being ready and willing to assist others in need. We must be especially careful not to serve only those who are important or powerful in the eyes of the world. It is the child, powerless, unimportant, having no status, on whom our eyes must be

[18]See e.g., Fleddermann, "Discipleship Discourse," 63.
[19]See Taylor, *St. Mark*, 305.

focused. To serve even a child, or especially a child, is to serve Jesus.

The radical nature of Jesus' teaching in these verses becomes clearer when we examine how the verb διακονεῖν (to serve) is used in the Greco-Roman world. At times it is used to refer specifically to male servants who wait on tables. When used in this manner, it speaks about an activity that is looked down upon as inappropriate behavior for a free man. In a more general sense, διακονεῖν means "to provide or care for" and is frequently used to refer to women's work.[20] Whether this refers to daily housework or to the raising of children, it is seen as activity unbecoming for a free man to perform.

When Jesus speaks about service, then, he is speaking about the kind of personal service that is rendered by one person to another person. It is reasonable to believe that Mark's audience would have understood this relationship between the one served and the server as a superior-subordinate relationship. As a result, this type of personal service would be considered inappropriate behavior for a free man in the Greco-Roman world. One of the requirements for following Jesus, therefore, is to engage in a type of activity considered by Greeks to be acceptable behavior only for women and servants.

Perhaps the type of service Jesus speaks of would be somewhat tolerable if performed for those who had wealth or status. It is conceivable that some benefits might accrue to the faithful servant of the rich and famous. But Jesus says that his followers must be servants of "all," even those completely without status or power in the Greco-Roman world, such as children (9:37). The result is that Jesus turns things upside down; he teaches that true greatness means giving yourself in personal service to one from whom you can receive no benefit in return. And, paradoxically, Mark informs his audience that it is in rendering such personal service to another that we meet Jesus and his Father (9:37).

---

[20]H. W. Beyer, "διακονέω," *TDNT* 2, 82.

The Third Discipleship Discourse (10:42-45)

Jesus and his disciples are nearing their destination and, in 10:32, we learn that they are on the road, going up to Jerusalem. Jesus is walking on ahead, leading the way, while those who follow him are said to be astonished and afraid. Immediately after this geographical notice Jesus utters his third and last passion-resurrection prediction (10:33-34). As in the previous two cases, once again Mark has followed Jesus' prediction of his coming death and resurrection with verses which show the inability of the disciples to understand what that means. As Jesus nears Jerusalem, soon to be the site of his own suffering and death, we find James and John, interested only in themselves, requesting places of special honor.

The request of the sons of Zebedee for precedence and rank provides another opportunity for Jesus to open the blind eyes of the disciples to the meaning of his suffering and death. Jesus suggests (1) that God, not he, will determine any such rankings (10:40), and (2) that the path to glory leads through suffering (10:38-39). This message is consistent with what we have seen elsewhere in the central section, especially in the three passion-resurrection predictions. The way of Jesus includes suffering and death prior to the glory of the resurrection. Those who wish to follow in his footsteps must be willing to travel along the same path that Jesus walked. Although they have journeyed with Jesus for some time now, James and John have yet to learn that the way of Jesus is the way of the cross.

Immediately following this exchange between Jesus and the sons of Zebedee, we find the final part of the now familiar pattern, the discipleship discourse. These verses (10:42-45), often seen as summarizing Mark's teaching on discipleship in the central section of his Gospel, constitute the third, and last, midsection discourse on discipleship and are followed only by the second half of the healing of the blind *inclusio*, the healing of Bartimaeus (10:46-52). This pericope is similar to the second discipleship discourse (9:35-37) in that the misunderstanding of the disciples is concerned with greatness or power and because Jesus contrasts the way of power and the way of service in his response. It is similar to the first passage (8:34–9:1) because it once again ties discipleship closely to the cross.

> **10** ⁴²And Jesus called them to him and said to them, "You know that those who are supposed to rule over the Gentiles lord it over them, and their great ones exercise authority over them. ⁴³But it shall not be so among you; but whoever would be great among you must be your servant, ⁴⁴and whoever would be first among you must be slave of all. ⁴⁵For the Son of Man also came not to be served but to serve, and to give his life as a ransom for many."

Jesus begins his remarks (10:42-45) by rejecting the way in which power is exercised in the Greco-Roman world in which he and his disciples live. The world labels as great those who dominate others, those who use their political or economic power to force the powerless to do their will. Frequently this kind of power leads to an abuse of the weak and defenseless so that the powerful might achieve their own ends. This worldly greatness is not to be the way of the disciples of Jesus. Followers of Jesus are to reverse this customary practice whereby those in authority rule by force. Those who wish to occupy leadership positions in the Christian community are informed that they are not to "lord it over" others or "exercise authority" over them. Mutuality and not dominance is called for in this radically "egalitarian ethos."[21]

The radical nature of the second midsection discipleship discourse (9:35-37) was seen when we examined the verb διακονέω (to serve) and discussed above what it might mean to "be last of all and servant of all" (9:35). The same requirement, to be a servant (διάκονος) is found here in the third discipleship discourse (10:43). In the parallel verse (10:44), however, Jesus uses even stronger language when he

---

[21]Donahue, *Discipleship in Mark*, 49. See also Best, "Mark's Use of the Twelve," 25 and Schweizer, *Good News*, 223.

informs his disciples that whoever would be first "must be slave (δοῦλος) of all" (10:44). Slaves were despised and rejected by both Jews and Greeks in the first century. They were considered to be property, on a lower level of humanity than those who were free.[22] Thus, this teaching of Jesus represents an especially dramatic reversal of worldly standards; Jesus truly has turned things upside down. The type of service Jesus requires of his followers is precisely that which was scorned and rejected by the world in which he lived.

Mark ends this pericope by having Jesus refer to the service that he himself will render by giving his life so that others might be free. There is little question in scholarly circles that the Suffering Servant of Isaiah 53 provides the background for Jesus' comment that the Son of Man came to give his life as "a ransom for many" (10:45; cf. Is 53:11-12). This will be discussed more thoroughly in chapter 7 below. It is enough to mention here that the Suffering Servant is really the model both for Jesus and for the community of disciples.

This emphasis on the ultimate sacrifice of Jesus reminds us of the earlier stated requirement of discipleship, carrying one's cross (8:34). Mark's interest in the "theology of the cross" should not blind us to the fact that one's greatness is not determined by how much one suffers. One's greatness, according to the last two discipleship discourses (9:35-37 and 10:42-45), depends on how much one serves. True discipleship, then, consists in giving of oneself in service to others. Helping others, rather than controlling them, is the mark of Christian discipleship.

Conclusion

When Jesus opens the eyes of Bartimaeus, who follows him on his way (10:52), he and his disciples are leaving Jericho. Now only fifteen miles from Jerusalem, the long journey they

---

[22]K. H. Rengstorf, "δοῦλος" *TDNT* 2, 261ff.

began at Caesarea Philippi is almost finished. Three times along the way from north to south Jesus has tried to open the eyes of the spiritually blind disciples. And three times these disciples have failed to understand that it was necessary for the Messiah to suffer and die. In the end, their eyes have not been opened to this new dimension of Messiahship.

This negative reaction of disciples to every announcement that Jesus' Messiahship includes suffering and death is not limited to the central section of Mark's Gospel. At the beginning of the Passion Narrative (14:1-11) we encounter the same theme. Jesus is sitting at the table in the house of Simon the leper when an unnamed woman pours costly ointment over Jesus' head. We soon learn that she has performed an act of prophetic anticipation because she has anointed his body "beforehand for burying" (14:8). This is the only anointing Jesus receives since the women who come to the tomb to anoint his corpse discover that he has already risen (16:1-6). Immediately after this obvious reference to the death of Jesus, we find another disciple who fails to understand, or refuses to accept, that Jesus must suffer and die. Judas Iscariot goes to the chief priests in order to betray Jesus to them. There are at least two possible ways to understand this: (1) Mark might want his readers to see Judas as so preoccupied with his own concerns that he fails to comprehend what has just happened. Thus, Judas' reaction to the announcement of Jesus' impending death would be similar to the disciples' reaction following the second and third passion-resurrection predictions. (2) Mark might want us to see in Judas someone who comprehends, at least partially, the meaning of the anointing and rejects this understanding of Messiahship. Thus, Judas' reaction would be similar to that of Peter in the first passion-resurrection prediction. In either case, once again we have the mention of Jesus' death followed by a less than acceptable reaction by one of his closest followers.

The insight that true discipleship involves service is also seen here in Mark 14:1-11. Jesus defends the service that this woman has rendered to him against the charges that this valuable ointment should have been sold and the proceeds given to the poor. He adds, "For you always have the poor with you, and whenever you will, you can do good to them; but you will not always have me" (14:7). This often misunderstood verse does not forbid helping the poor. On the contrary, since Mark's readers cannot anoint the body of Jesus, their responsibility, and ours, is to the poor. The post-resurrection disciple renders service to Jesus by serving the poor. This should remind us of the requirement, found in the second and third discipleship discourses, to be "servant of all" (9:35) or "slave of all" (10:44). In the Greco-Roman world, serving the poor would have been just as distasteful as serving children. But Jesus makes no racial, social, or sexual distinctions when he tells his disciples that it is everyone ("all") whom they must serve.

Jesus himself provides us with a model of this radical service when he dies on the cross so that others might be free. Would-be disciples must follow the way of Jesus, the way of the Suffering Servant who has come not to be served, but to serve.

4

The Markan Disciples and Discipleship

Thus far we have examined texts in which Jesus (a) called people to join him as his followers and (b) taught those who were following him on his way to Jerusalem about himself, his goal, and the meaning of discipleship. In the central section of the Gospel we saw that these intimate companions of Jesus never understood or accepted the fact that Jesus' Messiahship involved his suffering and death.[1] This insight should cause us to wonder about Mark's presentation of the disciples of Jesus in his Gospel. Does Mark intend these people to be models of Christian discipleship? If one wants to discover what it means to follow Jesus, should these intimate companions of Jesus serve as a guide?

The Negative Picture of the Disciples in Mark

As early as the first chapter of the Gospel (1:35-38) we see evidence that the relationship between Jesus and the indi-

---

[1]This is true within the frame of the Gospel, but not absolutely or permanently according to Christian tradition.

viduals he has just called to follow him is a bit strained.[2] Jesus separates himself from them to pray, but Simon and the others pursue him. When they find Jesus they suggest that he should stay at Capernaum because everyone is searching for him (1:37). The disciples' request is not in agreement with the purpose for which Jesus came. In order to successfully accomplish his mission, Jesus must travel and preach far beyond Capernaum (1:38). We see in the early part of the Gospel, therefore, the theme which we already know appears in the midsection of the Gospel; the disciples try to hold Jesus back and to divert him from his overall mission.

There is a similar problem at the Transfiguration, when Peter also tries to prevent Jesus from traveling on his "way" to the cross (9:2-8). After Jesus leads the Three (Peter, James, and John) up a high mountain and is transfigured before them (9:2), these disciples see Moses and Elijah conversing with Jesus (9:4). Peter responds to this experience of heavenly glory by saying to Jesus, "Let us make three booths, one for you and one for Moses and one for Elijah" (9:5). The fact that Peter wants to prolong this close association with the glorified Messiah, by building temporary dwelling places, suggests that once again (cf. 8:32) he is revolting against the idea of Messianic suffering.[3]

Throughout the first half of the Gospel (1:16–8:21), the disciples are unable to perceive who Jesus is. This is puzzling for readers of Mark's Gospel because these individuals continually witness Jesus' healings, exorcisms, and nature miracles. When he chooses the Twelve, Jesus gives them "authority to cast out demons" (3:15; 6:7), yet even after they use this power successfully (6:13) they still fail to understand

---

[2] A. Kuby, "Zur Konzeption des Markus-Evangeliums," *ZNW* 49 (1958) 55. Others who emphasize the negative portrait of the disciples in Mark are: J. B. Tyson, "The Blindness of the Disciples in Mark," *JBL* 80 (1961) 261-268; T. J. Weeden, *Mark: Traditions in Conflict* (Philadelphia: Fortress, 1971), and "The Heresy that Necessitated Mark's Gospel," *ZNW* 59 (1968) 145-158; and W. Kelber, *Kingdom*, "The Hour of the Son of Man and the Temptation of the Disciples," in *The Passion in Mark* (ed. W. Kelber; Philadelphia: Fortress, 1976) 41-60, and *Mark's Story of Jesus* (Philadelphia: Fortress, 1979).

[3] Taylor, *St. Mark*, 391, and Achtemeier, *Invitation*, 130-131.

Jesus, his mission, or what it means to follow him. In fact, in the verse which ends the first half of the Gospel (8:21) Jesus says to his disciples, "Do you still not understand?"

This summary verse appears in one of the four passages in the first half of the Gospel which include this motif (4:1-34; 6:45-52; 7:1-23; 8:14-21). In his first major speech (4:1-34) the Markan Jesus tells his disciples that they have "been given the secret of the Kingdom of God" (4:11). Yet these individuals who are closest to Jesus act more like the outsiders for whom "everything is in parables" (4:11), people who hear but do not understand (4:12). One would expect the disciples to be included among "the ones who hear the word and accept it and bear fruit" (4:20) yet Jesus says to them: "Do you not understand this parable? How then will you understand all the parables?" (4:13).

At the end of this speech about the mystery of the Kingdom of God, Jesus and his disciples depart in boats for the other side of the Sea of Galilee (4:35-41). During the trip across the lake a great storm arises and threatens to sink their boat (4:37). If they had recognized Jesus' ability to perform miracles it is reasonable to expect that they would have called out to him to use this power of his to rescue them from the dangers of the raging sea. This is not what happens, however, as the disciples demonstrate no faith in Jesus as the one who can save them.[4] They simply appear puzzled at Jesus' lack of concern about their predicament as they say, "Do you not care if we perish?" (4:38). Once awake, Jesus performs a powerful miracle in his stilling of the storm (4:39). The overall reaction of the disciples in this pericope, however, leads Jesus to ask them, "Have you no faith?" (4:40).

After the Feeding of the Five Thousand (6:32-44), Jesus makes his disciples get into a boat and head out before him to the other side of the lake. This pericope, usually referred to as The Walking on the Water (6:45-52), is the second of the four passages mentioned above as continuing the lack of understanding motif.

---

[4]Kuby, "Zur Konzeption," 56.

6 ⁴⁵Immediately he made his disciples get into the boat and go before him to the other side, to Bethsaida, while he dismissed the crowd. ⁴⁶And after he had taken leave of them, he went into the hills to pray. ⁴⁷And when evening came, the boat was out on the sea, and he was alone on the land. ⁴⁸And he saw that they were distressed in rowing, for the wind was against them. And about the fourth watch of the night he came to them, walking on the sea. He meant to pass by them, ⁴⁹but when they saw him walking on the sea they thought it was a ghost, and cried out; ⁵⁰for they all saw him, and were terrified. But immediately he spoke to them and said, "Take heart, it is I; have no fear." ⁵¹And he got into the boat with them and the wind ceased. And they were utterly astounded, ⁵²for they did not understand about the loaves, but their hearts were hardened.

The disciples are very much afraid when they see Jesus walking on the sea but he calms their fears as he reveals his identity (6:50) and gets into the boat with them. Instead of disciples who understand, however, we find disciples who are "utterly astonished" (6:51). And Mark tells us, in the last verse of this pericope, that the disciples "did not understand about the loaves" (6:52).

In the third failure to understand passage located in the first half of the Gospel (7:1-23), Jesus teaches about the traditional understanding of defilement and real defilement. The question is whether the Gentiles have to conform to Jewish practices, or whether Jesus has liberalized the tradition in order to make room for the Gentiles. In his answer, Jesus tells the crowd that the Jewish tradition is not just liberalized; it is no longer in force.⁵ After he enters the house and separates himself from the crowd, the disciples ask him about the parable he has just told. Jesus responds to their question by asking, "Then are you also without understanding?" (7:18).

Some of Jesus' harshest criticism is found in the fourth passage mentioned above, Mark's summary of Jesus' northern ministry (8:14-21).

⁵Kelber, *Kingdom*, 59.

8 [14]Now they had forgotten to bring bread; and they had only one loaf with them in the boat. [15]And he cautioned them, saying, "Take heed, beware of the leaven of the Pharisees and the leaven of Herod." [16]And they discussed it with one another, saying, "We have no bread." [17]And being aware of it, Jesus said to them, "Why do you discuss the fact that you have no bread? Do you not yet perceive or understand? Are your hearts hardened? [18]Having eyes do you not see, and having ears do you not hear? And do you not remember? [19]When I broke the five loaves for the five thousand, how many baskets full of broken pieces did you take up?" They said to him, "Twelve." [20]And the seven for the four thousand, how many baskets full of broken pieces did you take up?" And they said to him, "Seven." [21]And he said to them, "Do you not yet understand?"

The disciples seem to have missed the point of Jesus' words and deeds in the first half of the Gospel. He responds by saying, "Do you not perceive or understand? Are your hearts hardened? Having eyes do you not see, and having ears do you not hear?" (8:17-18). Jesus then reminds them of the two feeding miracles concluding "Do you not yet understand?" (8:21). In its present location, this question is immediately followed by the cure of the first blind man (8:22-25), and thus leads into the central section of the Gospel. What the disciples must understand, therefore, is seen in both the feeding stories and the central section of the Gospel.

It is impossible to deny that frequently the disciples fail to understand in the first half of Mark's Gospel (1:1–8:21). A startling change seems to take place in the perceptiveness of the disciples, however, as we begin the central section of this Gospel. In response to Jesus' question, "Who do you say that I am?" (8:29), Peter declares that Jesus is the Christ (8:29). This does not mean that Peter and the disciples now understand either Jesus' identity or his goal, as is quite clear in the verses which follow. When the midsection of the Gospel was examined above it was painfully revealed that whatever Peter's concept of messiahship is, it is not the same as Jesus' concept. These intimate followers of Jesus neither understand nor accept the concept of a suffering Messiah. What Peter's confession of Jesus as the Christ does mean, however, is that the disciples' lack of understanding has become misunderstanding. Because they now have an incorrect understanding of Jesus, they are unable to comprehend what he is telling them about the goal of his journey and the consequences of following him.

This same negative picture of the disciples also appears elsewhere in the central section of the Gospel. Between the first (8:31) and second (9:31) passion-resurrection predictions we find several passages in which the disciples are presented in an unfavorable light. (1) After Peter's negative actions at the Transfiguration (see above), Jesus and the Three descend the mountain (9:9ff.). (2) It is clear from the conversation which takes place as they are coming down the mountain that the disciples misunderstand about Elijah.

> **9** [9]And as they were coming down the mountain, he charged them to tell no one what they had seen, until the Son of Man should have risen from the dead. [10]So they kept the matter to themselves, questioning what the rising from the dead meant. [11]And they asked him, "Why do the scribes say that first Elijah must come?" [12]And he said to them, "Elijah does come first to restore all things; and how is it written of the Son of Man, that he should suffer many things and be treated with contempt? [13]But I tell you that Elijah has come, and they did to him whatever they pleased, as it is written of him."

First century Judaism understood Malachi 4:4-5 to mean that Elijah would appear before the coming of the Messiah.[6] Jesus accepts this, indicates that Elijah has already come in the person of John the Baptist, and adds that the suffering and death of the forerunner at the hands of the violent was foretold in Scripture (9:12-13; cf. 1 Kgs. 19:2, 10). If what

---

[6]Nineham, *Saint Mark*, 239; Schweizer, *Good News*, 184-185; and Achtemeier, *Invitation*, 132.

Scripture has said about John/Elijah has been fulfilled, then one should expect that what Scripture says about the suffering of the Son of Man will also be fulfilled (9:12). We should not forget that Mark has already presented both Jesus' words about the suffering of the Son of Man (8:31) and God's words urging disciples to listen to Jesus (9:7). Mark has once again emphasized the suffering of Jesus and the incomprehension of the disciples. (3) After Jesus, Peter, James and John join the rest of the disciples (9:14), a discussion ensues in which it is revealed that Jesus' disciples were unable to perform an exorcism (9:18) because of their lack of faith (cf. 9:29).[7]

Mark continues to emphasize this motif as he presents the disciples in a negative light on several occasions between the second (9:31) and third (10:33-34) passion-resurrection predictions. (1) When he learns that his disciples have forbidden an individual, who was not of their company, from casting out demons in his name (9:38-41), Jesus responds by saying, "Do not forbid him; for no one who does a mighty work in my name will be able soon after to speak evil of me" (9:39). (2) Mark tells us that Jesus was "indignant" (10:14-15) when he learned that his disciples were trying to keep children away from him (10:13). The disciples should have known better, since Jesus previously had embraced a child in their midst (9:36f.; cf. 10:16). (3) The fact that the disciples are "amazed" (10:24) and "exceedingly astonished" (10:26) at Jesus' words, about the relationship between riches and the Kingdom of God, contributes to the negative image one has of these followers of Jesus.

This negative picture of the disciples, found both in the first half of the Gospel and in the central section of the Gospel, also appears in the dialogue on Peter's denial (14:26-31) and in the Gethsemane episode (14:32-42).

---

[7]Understood in this way by Schweizer, *Good News*, 188, and Achtemeier, *Invitation*, 135, although it is not clear to whom the words about the "faithless generation" (9:19) refer.

²⁶And when they had sung a hymn, they went out to the Mount of Olives. ²⁷And Jesus said to them, "You will all fall away; for it is written, 'I will strike the shepherd, and the sheep will be scattered.' ²⁸But after I am raised up, I will go before you to Galilee." ²⁹Peter said to him, "Even though they all fall away, I will not." ³⁰And Jesus said to him, "Truly, I say to you, this very night, before the cock crows twice, you will deny me three times." ³¹But he said vehemently, "If I must die with you, I will not deny you." And they all said the same.

This exchange between Jesus and Peter prior to the Gethsemane scene clearly portrays Peter in an unfavorable light. Jesus informs his disciples that they all will fall away, just as Scripture (Zech. 13:7) has predicted. Peter refuses to accept Jesus' words, just as he apparently has refused to accept that Scripture was fulfilled in the suffering and death of John the Baptist (9:13) and that Scripture will be fulfilled in the suffering and death of the Son of Man (8:31; 9:12, 31; 10:33-34). Jesus responds to Peter's statement, "Even though they all fall away, I will not" (14:29) by predicting precisely how Peter will fulfill the prophecy (i.e., by denial). Peter's "vehement" objection only serves to reinforce our negative picture of him and the other disciples (10:31). In the Gethsemane pericope, which follows immediately after this dialogue, Jesus tells his disciples to sit and wait for him while he goes off to pray; but he takes his three most intimate companions, Peter, James, and John, with him. These three form an inner group among the Twelve in Mark's Gospel. They are the only disciples (a) to be given new names by Jesus (3:16-17), (b) whom Jesus allows to accompany him when he enters Jairus' house to revive his daughter (5:37ff.), (c) who journey up the mountain with Jesus and witness his Transfiguration (9:2-13), (d) whom Jesus takes with him as he separates from the others in Gethsemane, and who, together with Andrew, (e) are the first disciples called to follow Jesus (1:16-20) and (f) the only disciples who speak privately with Jesus as he sits on the Mount of Olives after having predicted the destruction of the Temple buildings (13:3ff.). These are the three disciples Jesus asks to support him by watching and praying as he goes a short distance from them to pray in the place called Gethsemane (14:32-42). Three times he separates from them to pray, and each time he returns he finds them sleeping.

The situation only gets worse as the disciple Judas betrays Jesus (14:43ff.), all flee at his arrest (14:50), and Peter adamantly denies that he ever knew Jesus (14:66-72). Some would add that the Gospel ends emphasizing the failure of Jesus' disciples. The women who receive the message of the resurrection (16:6) fail to tell the other disciples because they are afraid (16:7-8).[8]

Mark's generally negative portrait of the disciples should not blind us to their positive attributes. In spite of all their shortcomings, the disciples of Jesus appear to believe that he has something to offer them for which it is worthwhile to leave all and follow him. They abandon everything, their occupations, relatives, and acquaintances, in response to his call (1:16-20). And when Peter reminds Jesus of this fact (10:28), Jesus does not deny it, but assures them that they will be rewarded (10:29-30). Although they never fully understand Jesus, his goal, or the demands of discipleship, they do remain with him until his arrest (14:50).

The disciples seem to comprehend something about Jesus' power since they tell him about Peter's mother-in-law's illness (1:30) and are not said to be amazed when Jesus cures her (cf. 1:27). It is not reported that they are surprised when Jesus gives them "authority over the unclean spirits" (6:7-13). And James and John assume that Jesus has the power and authority needed to insure them positions of precedence in his "glory" (10:35ff.).

Even pericopes which appear at first to view the disciples in a positive light often end by highlighting their darker side

<hr>

[8]N. Perrin, *The Resurrection According to Matthew, Mark and Luke* (Philadelphia: Fortress, 1977) 31; Weeden, *Traditions*, 47-50, 102-111; and Kelber, *Kingdom*, 146, and "Apostolic Tradition and the Form of the Gospel," in *Discipleship in the New Testament* (ed. F. F. Segovia; Philadelphia: Fortress, 1985) 36.

however. The "success story" of the mission of the Twelve (6:7-13, 30) surrounds the story of the death of John the Baptist (6:14-29), clearly intended to foreshadow the fate of Jesus himself. Because Mark tells the story in this manner, a shadow is cast on the positive response to their message. In the pericope which follows their return, the Feeding of the Five Thousand, there seems to be a strong contrast between Jesus' concern for the crowd and the disciples' request that he "send them away" (6:36). It is as if the disciples have missed the point of their own mission, as well as of Jesus' mission and identity.

It is clear, therefore, that the picture Mark paints of the disciples of Jesus is a complex one. Having both positive and negative features, they are presented by Mark sometimes in a favorable, but more often in an unfavorable, light. There have been various scholarly responses to this portrayal of the disciples. Of those who highlight the negative aspect of the disciples in Mark, Theodore J. Weeden[9] and Werner H. Kelber[10] are the most persistent, consistent, and controversial. Weeden argues that there is a progression in Mark from the disciples' imperception of Jesus' miraculous powers (1:1-8:26) to their misunderstanding of the necessity of suffering in the Messiahship of Jesus (8:27-10:52) to their outright denial and rejection of the suffering, dying Messiah. He believes that Mark is using the disciples as tools in an attack against a false Christology in his own church. According to Weeden, Jesus is seen by some in the Markan community as a θεῖος 'ανήρ (divine man) who had descended to earth with supernatural power. This understanding of Jesus leads Mark's opponents to focus on the promises Jesus made to his followers about their full participation in his power. Peter and the disciples, then, are seen as representatives of this group that emphasizes

---

[9]"The Heresy That Necessitated Mark's Gospel," and *Traditions*.

[10]*Kingdom*, idem, "Mark 14:32-42: Gethsemane," *ZNW* 63 (1972) 166-87; idem, "The Hour," 41-60; idem, *Mark's Story of Jesus*, idem, *The Oral and the Written Gospel: The Hermeneutics of Speaking and Writing in the Synoptic Tradition, Mark, Paul, and Q* (Philadelphia: Fortress, 1983) 90-139; and idem, "Apostolic Tradition," 24-46.

glory (transfiguration, resurrection) rather than the cross. Mark is said to attack this position by his negative picture of the disciples, his stress on suffering and the theology of the cross, and his lack of a resurrection appearance. What results from this approach is the conclusion that Mark has written his Gospel specifically to have Jesus reject the disciples and their erroneous Christology. The failure of the Markan disciples is a direct result of their heretical Christology. Mark and his supporters would then have been able to use this Gospel to combat the Christological heresy raging in their own community.[11]

Kelber also focuses on the negative picture of the Markan disciples, but he identifies the heresy as a false eschatology.[12] He believes that the Gospel was written shortly after 70 A.D. in response to a crisis in the Christian community caused by the fall of Jerusalem and the destruction of the Temple. Prior to 70 A.D. the Jerusalem Church, with its apostolic leadership, is said to have been looking forward to the imminent coming of the apocalyptic Son of Man from heaven mentioned in Daniel 7:13-14. Their hopes for the return of Jesus as the Son of Man were destroyed together with Jerusalem and its Temple in the disastrous war with Rome. Mark's Gospel is then seen as providing hope to those caught up in this disaster by pointing out that the Kingdom of God was never intended to arrive with the destruction of Jerusalem (claimed by the false prophets of 13:5-6, 21-22). The Markan Jesus teaches the correct eschatology which points to the near future in Galilee

[11]For a critical evaluation of this position see e.g., O. Betz, "The Concept of the So-Called 'Divine Man' in Mark's Christology," in *Studies in New Testament and Early Christian Literature* (NovTSup 33, ed. D. E. Aune; Leiden: Brill, 1972) 229-240; W. L. Lane, "*Theios Anēr* Christology and the Gospel of Mark," in *New Dimensions in New Testament Study* (ed. R. N. Longenecker and M.C. Tenney; Grand Rapids: Zondervan, 1974) 144-161; C.R. Holladay, *Theios Anēr* in *Hellenistic Judaism: A Critique of the Use of this Category in New Testament Christology* (SBLDS 40; Missoula: Scholars, 1977); and Kelber, "Apostolic Tradition," 28.

[12]In his recent works, *The Oral and the Written Gospel*, 199-211, and "Apostolic Tradition," 41-42, Kelber argues that Mark presents the disciples in a negative light in an attempt to undermine and correct an oral tradition "fraught with gnosticizing proclivities."

(16:6-8) as the time and place for his return. Jerusalem was never intended to be the site of the parousia. The founding of the Jerusalem Church was a mistake, and against the wishes of Jesus. If the women who went to the tomb had done as they were instructed and communicated to the disciples the message given to them by the young man in the white robe, the focus of the first Christians would not have been on Jerusalem at all, but on Galilee (16:7-8). Mark argues against those who believed that Jesus would return to Jerusalem immediately after the destruction of the Temple. Gaililee, and not Jerusalem, is the place where the parousia will take place. He gives hope to his readers as he points out that they still have time to journey to Galilee before the imminent return of Jesus. They must start out "on the way" to Galilee where the Kingdom soon will make its appearance.

The conclusions of Kelber and Weeden, who explain the negative picture of the disciples in Mark as a polemic against opponents in the Markan community, have not met with widespread acceptance in scholarly circles.[13] The two reasons cited most often are: (1) the lack of external evidence of the existence of such opponents, and (2) the positive features of the disciples and positive theology of discipleship in Mark.

Another group of scholars also recognizes Mark's negative presentation of the disciples, but thinks that the interpretations of Kelber and Weeden have carried the evidence too far. Ernest Best[14] admits that Mark presents a negative picture of the disciples, but claims this is due primarily to the fact that everyone knew the basic traditions about the disciples, especially Peter and Judas. Because of the known facts Mark is constrained. He cannot picture the disciples as receiving sight prior to the resurrection. What Mark does, therefore, is use the disciples in order to illustrate to his readers the true meaning of discipleship. The Markan community is pictured as focusing primarily on the miraculous powers of Jesus and

---

[13]See e.g., P. J. Achtemeier, *Mark* (2nd rev. ed., Proclamation Commentaries; Philadelphia: Fortress, 1986) 105-113; E. Best, "The Role," 377-401; and Donahue, *Discipleship in Mark*, 24-31.

[14]*Following*, 136-137.

the resulting benefits for the individual Christian and the community. Mark wants to point out that the disciple is not one who only has to sit back and reap the benefits of being a Christian; the cross of Christ presents a missionary challenge to all would-be followers of the risen Lord. The result of telling the story this way is that Mark presents Christian discipleship in terms of stages. The initial reaction to the charismatic activity of Jesus, which emphasizes his miraculous powers, is followed by a late appreciation of the centrality of the cross to true discipleship. Because stage two happened only after the resurrection for the historical disciples it could not be narrated in the Gospel. Mark has preserved the material dealing with the necessity of suffering so that his readers, who live in the post-resurrection era, can more easily be brought to this second stage. Mark's goal, therefore, is to instruct his own community about the nature of Jesus' suffering and the likelihood of their own.

Somewhat similar to Best's approach is the literary analysis approach of Robert C. Tannehill.[15] According to Tannehill, it is reasonable to assume that the Christian readers of Mark's Gospel would have identified with the disciples, those who respond positively to Jesus. Mark anticipates and reinforces this identification by initially presenting the disciples in a favorable light. From the beginning of the Gospel through 6:30, the disciples for the most part, are viewed positively.[16] As the story progresses, however, they gradually come into conflict with Jesus on important issues. Because their response is seen as inadequate a real tension develops for the readers. The disciples become disastrous failures and the readers are forced to distance themselves from the disciples. A choice must be made between Jesus, with his difficult demands, and the disciples, with whom the readers have formed a positive attachment. Mark tells the story in this manner because he wants his readers to reflect on their own understanding of

---

[15]"Narrative Role." Sometimes called narrative analysis/criticism, Tannehill's approach plays an important part in Kelber's most recent studies.

[16]Ibid., 398.

Jesus, his mission, and Christian discipleship. Ultimately, Mark expects this self-examination will force his readers to change their attitudes and behavior. Those who so closely resemble Jesus' disciples as portrayed in Mark's Gospel will realize that the path they have chosen is in conflict with the way of Jesus.

Conclusion

What can we conclude from this representative sample of scholarly opinions? (1) The importance of the "way" motif is generally accepted, (2) as is the importance of Mark's "theology of the cross." (3) The disciples of Jesus are seen in a negative light throughout much, if not most, of the Gospel. (4) Therefore, any positive attraction the reader has to the disciples is, or ought to be, tempered by the misunderstanding of these initial followers of Jesus. (5) Since Mark certainly would claim to understand the way of discipleship, and to be making that understanding available to his readers he should be seen as using the difficulties of the disciples to provide his readers with an object lesson in how *not* to understand discipleship and Jesus. (6) The disciples' problems provide Mark with the opportunity to emphasize what he thinks is especially important. As we have seen already, and will develop more fully below, the would-be disciple must follow Jesus in order to come to understand who Jesus is. The one who travels along the way of Jesus gradually comes to understand Jesus' identity, the necessity of his suffering and death, and what significance these have for the correct understanding and practice of discipleship.

In order to arrive at this last conclusion one must see the story of Jesus and his disciples continuing beyond the last verse of the Gospel (16:8). It was admitted above that within the frame of the Gospel, the disciples do not arrive at a correct understanding of Jesus or Christian discipleship. There are several indications within the Gospel itself, however, which suggest that Mark did expect his readers/hearers to see the successful resolution of the disciples' dilemma as taking place in the post-resurrection era.[17] (1) Mark informs us that, as Jesus, Peter, James, and John, were coming down the mountain after the Transfiguration, Jesus "charged them to tell no one what they had seen, until the Son of Man should have risen from the dead" (9:9). Regardless of whether this refers to the resurrection or the parousia, it clearly looks forward to a fulfillment after Mark 16:8. (2) Tannehill, while insisting that we pay close attention to Mark's narrative, concludes that Jesus' discourse in Mark 13 "anticipates a continuing role for the disciples beyond the disaster of chapter 14."[18] (3) Mark presents Jesus himself looking forward to a post-resurrection meeting with his disciples as he says, "But after I am raised up, I will go before you to Galilee" (14:28). (4) These words of Jesus are recalled in 16:7 when the "young man" in the white robe says to the women who had come to anoint Jesus, "Tell his disciples and Peter that he is going before you to Galilee; there you will see him, as he told you." The best conclusion, therefore, is that while in the Gospel Mark presents the disciples as not understanding or accepting the fact that Jesus' Messiahship involved his suffering and death, he did not intend this to imply an absolute or permanent misunderstanding.

[17]See N.R. Petersen, *Literary Criticism for New Testament Critics* (GBS; Philadelphia: Fortress, 1978) 79. This is also the position of Best, Boomershine, Schmahl, Stock, and many others. For an opposing view see Kelber, "Apostolic Tradition."

[18]"Narrative Role," 402.

5

Discipleship and Community

Although the dynamic nature of Christian discipleship is obvious to most readers of the New Testament, there have been some over the centuries who have read these texts as supporting theological individualism. They claim that Jesus is appealing to the soul of each individual and that he is calling people exclusively as individuals to an invisible discipleship of the heart. What is sometimes called the "vertical dimension of discipleship," the relationship between the individual and Jesus or God, is thus seen as the essence of Christian discipleship. If this conclusion is one's starting point, then it is possible to read a number of the texts we have examined as supporting this position. Jesus calls an ordinary individual, who is going about his/her normal daily activities, to leave all and follow him on his way. Nothing must stand in the way of this exclusive relationship with Jesus, neither possessions, nor occupation, nor relatives. The person who accepts this call is to trust Jesus and develop a deep personal relationship with him.

This focus on the vertical dimension of discipleship, the individual's own personal call and subsequent relationship with the Lord, can easily lead to selfishness and a lack of concern for others. It has appeared in different forms in some

Reformation churches and in the Catholic church. In some of the Reformation churches this position appears as an extreme version of "justification by faith alone." "Faith," defined essentially as "trust," is seen as all important while "good works" are viewed as unimportant and unnecessary. All too often this emphasis on total confidence in God, who is in control of everything has led individuals to see their own human activity as unimportant and to lose any sense of responsibility for the future of the world. This understanding of Christian discipleship, which virtually ignores the injustices in the world, has been challenged by scholars in the same Reformation tradition. Dietrich Bonhoeffer, the famous Lutheran pastor who died a martyr's death at the hands of the Nazis at the end of World War II, calls this exclusive emphasis on the internal state of the individual "cheap grace."[1] He argues that Christian discipleship involves more than simply passive acceptance of salvation won by Christ. If the external acts of the individual are unimportant then neither contrition nor a desire to amend one's ways is necessary. Bonhoeffer believes that this is contrary to the teaching of the New Testament, which clearly requires obedience to the word of God. True grace is "costly" not "cheap." It involves the conversion of the whole person. It means giving oneself totally and completely to Christ. John Reumann, a modern Lutheran biblical scholar, essentially agrees when he states that post-biblical interpretation has often robbed "faith" of its biblical meaning of obedience as well as trust.[2] Any definition of faith that does not include the active, joyous, serving response to the will of God is a distortion of the New Testament understanding of faith.

In the Catholic church this theological individualism has appeared whenever the primary focus of attention has been either: (1) "the immediate relationship of the soul to God in a contemplative union that can best be achieved through

---

[1] *The Cost of Discipleship* (rev. ed. trans. R. H. Fuller; New York: Macmillan, 1963) 45ff.

[2] *Jesus In The Church's Gospels* (Philadelphia: Fortress, 1968) 169ff.

relative detachment from the world."[3] or (2) "an assent to a determinate body of revealed doctrine." Whenever the first situation occurs, the individual is so preoccupied with contemplation that there is little or no interest in social or economic problems and no intense human concern for the well being of others.

> Man is seen as essentially an intellectual being, having as his chief end an act of contemplative knowledge. The contemplative life is viewed as per se superior to the active life. As a result the believer is constantly drawn toward a certain spiritual hedonism. The long prevalence of this doctrine of faith is reckoned among the principal causes of the split between faith and the daily life of the Christian, which Vatican II, in its *Pastoral Constitution on the Church in the Modern World*, signalized as one of the more serious errors of our age (n. 43).[4]

Whenever the second situation occurs, we find the believer so concerned with guaranteed propositions of faith that he/she fails to see the religious significance of working for justice here on earth.

> Salvation is sought by preference in the ecclesiastical sphere of sacred doctrine and worship rather than in the secular sphere of economic or political life. This false orientation, so easily arising out of the assent theory of faith, is of course at the root of the charges that Christianity alienates man from his proper task and lures him into an illusory world of transcendental irresponsibility.[5]

In order to combat this danger of interpreting Christian discipleship as a private, internal matter, we have suggested

---

[3]The insights in this paragraph are those of A. Dulles, "The Meaning of Faith Considered in Relationship to Justice," in *The Faith That Does Justice* (ed. J. C. Haughey; New York: Paulist, 1977) 10-46, especially 14-22.

[4]*Ibid.*, 17.

[5]*Ibid.*, 19-20.

above that there is also a "horizontal dimension to discipleship." The gracious invitation to follow Jesus involves following his example of service to others, especially the poor and those encountered in the missionary enterprise. Following Jesus means following his example of "bearing good fruit." Christian discipleship, as we have seen, is dynamic and involves being of service to others. While the right intention of the individual is important, to conclude that this is all that Jesus demands is to reduce the teaching of Jesus to harmless platitudes. Jesus clearly calls upon those who would be his followers to actually "do" the will of God (3:35).[6]

We now have some understanding of Mark's teaching on discipleship, yet because our picture is still incomplete we too run the risk of focusing exclusively on the individual. It is possible to admit that good works, should or must flow from one's total commitment to follow Jesus, and still overlook or dismiss the notion of community in the New Testament. The church is neither (1) a loosely associated group of well-meaning individuals nor (2) a loosely associated group of well-meaning individuals who, quite independently, often bear good fruit. There is a communal dimension to Christian discipleship which must not be ignored.

When scholars discuss this communal aspect of Christian discipleship they frequently point to Matthew and Luke, rather than to Mark. Matthew's interest in this facet of discipleship is evident as (1) he includes a discourse by Jesus on community life in chapter 18 of his Gospel, and (2) he is the only evangelist to use of the technical term ἐκκλησία or "church" (16:18; 18:17), in his Gospel. While Luke does portray the followers of Jesus as gathered together (24:33) and spending time together at the Jerusalem Temple (24:52) in his Gospel, the most obvious example of Luke's interest in community appears in his second volume, The Acts of the Apostles. The disciples of Jesus are said to be of "one accord" as they pray together (Acts 1:14) and to be of "one heart and soul" as they live in common, their generosity insuring that

---

[6]See e.g., G. Lohfink, *Jesus and Community*, 58.

there will be no needy among them (Acts 4:32; 2:44-45). The earliest word that Luke uses to designate this group which gathered together for apostolic instruction, fellowship, prayer, and the breaking of bread (Acts 2:42ff.) is κοινωνία (association, communion, or fellowship). Beginning in Acts 5:11, however, Luke uses ἐκκλησία, "church," to describe the early Christian community. It is unlikely that one would find many references to Mark's Gospel in any discussion about the communal dimension of Christian discipleship, yet we believe that Mark agrees with the other evangelists and understands that the communal nature of discipleship is of crucial importance.[7]

The Community Exists

Two of the most important pericopes for our discussion of discipleship and community are texts dealing with the family of Jesus (3:20-35; 10:28ff.), which we have referred to above. Prior to Jesus' first major speech in Mark, there is a lengthy section (3:20-35)[8] which often provokes heated discussion among readers of this Gospel.

> **3** [19]Then he went home; [20]and the crowd came together again, so that they could not even eat. [21]And when his family heard it, they went out to seize him, for they said, "He is beside himself." [22]And the scribes who came down from Jerusalem said, "He is possessed by Beelzebub, and by the prince of demons he casts out the demons."
>
> [31]And his mother and his brothers came; and standing outside they sent to him and called him. [32]And a crowd was sitting about him; and they said to him, "Your mother and your brothers are outside, asking for you." [33]And he

---

[7]J.A., Estrada Díaz, "Las relaciones Jesús-pueblo-discípulos en el evangelio de Marcos," *Estudios Eclesiásticos* 54 (1979) 162; Best, *Following*, 208-245; Donahue, *Discipleship in Mark*, 31-51; and Lohfink, *Jesus and Community*.

[8]On the unity of this section see Schweizer, *Good News*, 82-84.

replied, "Who are my mother and my brothers?"[34] And
looking around on those who sat about him, he said, "Here
are my mother and my brothers! [35]Whoever does the will of
God is my brother, and sister, and mother."

As this passage begins we learn (1) that certain people,
referred to as οἱ παρ' αὐτοῦ ("his own"), go out to seize Jesus
because "they" are saying that he is "beside himself" (3:20-21).
Immediately following these verses is a dialogue (2) between
Jesus and the Jerusalem scribes in which they accuse Jesus of
being possessed by Satan. Jesus responds with comments
about the divided house, the divided kingdom, and the sin
against the Holy Spirit (3:22-30). (3) The section ends when
Jesus' mother and brothers come asking for him and Jesus
defines what it means to be a member of his family (3:31-35).

There are several questions which must be answered about
this passage: (a) Who are "his own"? (b) What is the
relationship between "his own" (vs. 21) and Jesus' mother and
brothers (vs. 31ff.)? (c) Who claims Jesus is "beside himself"?
(d) What does being "beside himself" mean?

While it is possible to translate οἱ παρ' αὐτοῦ as either "his
friends," "those who were customarily around him," or "his
family," scholars generally agree that Mark understood this
phrase as referring to Jesus' relatives from Nazareth.[9] The
widely recognized Markan use of intercalation (mentioned
earlier) is apparent here and supports this conclusion. Mark
has inserted the story about the scribes from Jerusalem (3:22-
30) in between these two sections concerning the family of
Jesus (3:20-21 and 3:31-35). Although those who claim Jesus
is "beside himself" are referred to simply as "they," most
believe that Mark intends the reader to understand that this is
the same group referred to earlier in verse 21, οἱ παρ' αὐτοῦ.
Therefore, it is the family of Jesus that declares him to be out
of his mind or mentally deranged.[10]

---

[9]See e.g., Taylor, *Mark*, 236-237; Kelber, *Kingdom*, 25; and R. E. Brown, et al.
Mary in the New Testament (Philadelphia: Fortress; New York: Paulist, 1978) 54ff.

[10]Ibid. See also Lohfink, *Jesus and Community*, 42-43, and Donahue,
Discipleship in Mark, 33.

The most important verses for us in this large passage are the final ones in which Jesus explains who it is that really constitutes his family (3:31-35). As the scene opens, we find Jesus inside a house with a crowd "sitting about him." His own mother and brothers are said to be "standing outside" (vss. 31, 32). According to Mark, Jesus makes a clear distinction between those who are inside and those who are outside, identifying "those who sat about him" (vs. 34) as his true relatives, his new family.[11] "Whoever does the will of God" is Jesus' brother, sister, and mother (vs. 35).

There is some disagreement among scholars concerning exactly how Mark understands Jesus' relationship to his natural family. Those mentioned earlier who highlight the negative picture of the disciples usually argue that Mark's attitude toward the natural family of Jesus is similar to his attitude toward the disciples who, according to them, represent a heretical theology.[12] Mark is seen as joining the hostility of the Jerusalem scribes and the hostility of Jesus' relatives by means of his intercalation technique. Others adopt a more moderate position and argue that the passage does not exclude the members of Jesus' natural family from eventually participating in this new community composed of those who do the will of God.[13] Mark's main intent, they say, is not to exclude Jesus' natural family from his community of disciples, but to define clearly what is required for one to participate in this community. What is important for us, and something on which both groups of scholars can agree, is that the natural family of Jesus has no real importance in the new community established by Jesus' proclamation of the Kingdom of God. Whether or not one is biologically or naturally related to Jesus is irrelevant; what matters is whether or not one is obedient to the will of God. As Jesus says quite clearly, "whoever does the will of God" (3:35) has fulfilled the requirement for membership in his eschatological family.

---

[11]Kelber, *Kingdom*, 25-26; Lohfink, *Jesus and Community*, 43; Donahue, *Discipleship in Mark*, 32-34; and Brown, *Mary*, 53f.

[12]Weeden, *Traditions*, 23-51, and Kelber, *Kingdom*, 25-27.

[13]Brown, *Mary*, 53.

obedient to the will of God. As Jesus says quite clearly, "whoever does the will of God" (3:35) has fulfilled the requirement for membership in his eschatological family.

When Jesus identifies those sitting about him who do the will of God as his mother, brothers, and sisters it is implicit that these disciples are also mothers, brothers, and sisters to one another. This new relationship among Jesus' disciples becomes explicit in the second important passage dealing with the new family of Jesus (10:28ff.). Let us recall briefly the wider context of this passage. This text about the community of disciples appears in the famous central section of the Gospel, portions of which we have discussed earlier. The immediate context of these verses (10:29-31) is the private instruction Jesus gives to his disciples after the story of the rich man (10:17ff.). As Jesus is traveling on his way from Galilee to Jerusalem he encounters a rich man who asks what he must do to inherit eternal life. Although this man has fulfilled the requirement of the Jewish law he is not accepted by Jesus. The man goes away very sad when he realizes that he is unable to do what Jesus asks him to do—sell what he has, give to the poor, and follow Jesus. His refusal, because of his "many possessions" (10:22), results in Jesus making a comment to his disciples about the virtual impossibility of a rich person entering the Kingdom of God (10:23ff.). The disciples then ask Jesus how anyone can be saved (10:26) and he reminds them of the absolute gratuity of salvation when he says that "all things are possible with God" (10:27). Immediately following this, Peter reminds Jesus that he and the others have left everything in order to follow Jesus (10:28). Jesus responds:

> **10** [29]"Truly, I say to you, there is no one who has left house or brothers or sisters or mother or father or children or lands, for my sake and for the gospel, [30]who will not receive a hundredfold now in this time, houses and brothers and sisters and mothers and children and lands, with persecutions, and in the age to come eternal life."

Mark seems to draw a parallel between this rich man and the disciples, suggesting that the "many possessions" which could get in the way of true discipleship are house, brothers, sisters, mother, father, children, or lands (10:30). As we have seen earlier, a complete renunciation of one's former way of life is demanded.[14] The difficulty of doing what Jesus requires should not be passed over lightly. The brothers and sisters one may be called to leave behind are blood relatives with whom, in all likelihood, the individual has shared the joys and sorrows of childhood and young adulthood. They are a source of support and protection. The mother and father that the disciple may have to separate from in order to follow Jesus are the objects of one of the most important of the ten commandments, "Honor your father and your mother, that your days may be long in the land which the Lord your God gives you" (Ex. 20:12). In Israelite society the parents are seen as partners with God in giving the child life and they provide the care and sustenance necessary during the child's formative years. The suggestion that one might have to leave behind one's children is just as startling, since children were seen as a source of great joy and were expected to care for their aging parents. The house and fields one might have to leave behind are best seen as part of the family inheritance which the faithful Israelite is obliged to maintain. Thus Jesus has declared that in order to be his disciple one might have to leave all those people and possessions which formerly offered support, sustenance, protection, and life itself.

Those who follow Jesus, who leave everything behind in order to do the will of God, are promised by Jesus that they will have, "in this time," new houses, brothers, sisters, mothers, children, and lands. This obviously points to the existence of a new family, a new community.

There are a number of insights one can get from these verses into Mark's understanding of this community. (1) When we compare the list of what one might have to give up

---

[14]Best, *Following*, 113; Kelber, *Kingdom*, 87-89; and Donahue, *Discipleship in Mark*, 37-46.

in order to follow Jesus with the list of what one will gain by following him, we notice that the two lists are not identical. By adding "persecutions" (10:30) to the things that the faithful follower of Jesus will receive, Mark has once again drawn our attention to the importance of the suffering of Jesus and those who choose to go after him. One must follow Jesus for the right reasons, therefore, and not because one expects life will be more enjoyable and filled only with pleasant rewards.

Missing entirely from both these lists in Mark's Gospel is (2) "wife" (cf. Luke 18:29). There has been much speculation about this, but the most common suggestions are: (a) that the marriage bond was seen as so important that nothing short of martyrdom could justify the permanent breaking of it[15] or (b) that the idea of many wives could only be misunderstood.[16] There is at least one other possibility, however, that is worth considering. If, as we have suggested above, Mark understands the female followers of Jesus to be disciples (15:41), then it is possible that he has intentionally omitted both "wives" and "husbands" from his lists. The result is that the references to what might have to be left behind could apply equally as well to either female or male disciples. The women who followed Jesus also had to be willing to leave behind "house or brothers or sisters or mother or father or children or lands" for Jesus' sake and for the gospel (10:29).

Perhaps the most interesting thing about these two lists is (3) the fact that the term "father," included in what one might have to give up, is omitted from the list of relatives one will gain from following Jesus. The absence of a new "father," in the new community (vs. 30) has usually been understood to be because the disciple has only one father, God.[17] But it is also possible that the term "fathers" is too symbolic of patriarchal domination and Mark's view of the Christian community is much more egalitarian.[18]

---

[15]Nineham, *Saint Mark*, 276.

[16]Achtemeier, *Invitation*, 151.

[17]Best, *Following*, 114.

[18]Lohfink, *Jesus and Community*, 44-50, and Donahue, *Discipleship in Mark*, 43.

In Judaism the father of the family had the right to demand honor and obedience. His authority was absolute; it could not be questioned.[19] This is the same type of domination Jesus speaks against in Mark 10:42-45 when he points out that it is the Gentiles who rule by force and by dominating others. Jesus clearly tells his disciples that "it shall not be so among you." Domination of others, whether the model is the Gentile civil authorities or the traditional patriarch, is simply not permitted in the new family of Jesus. The misuse of ecclesiastical position and power is just as detestable as the misuse of political or economic power by secular authorities.

Mark's emphasis on the communal nature of Christian discipleship is also seen at the end of Jesus' second major speech in this Gospel:

> **13** [33]Take heed, watch; for you do not know when the time will come. [34]It is like a man going on a journey, when he leaves home and puts his servants in charge, each with his or her own work, and commands the doorkeeper to be on the watch. [35]Watch therefore—for you do not know when the master of the house will come, in the evening, or at midnight, or at cockcrow, or in the morning—[36]lest he come suddenly and find you asleep. [37]And what I say to you I say to all: Be on Guard!"

Although in its present context this speech could be seen as addressed only to Peter, James, John, and Andrew (13:3-4), it is clear that Mark intended his readers to see themselves included in the $\pi\hat{\alpha}\sigma\iota\nu$ ("all") of the final verse: "What I say to you, I say to all: Be on Guard!" (13:37).[20] Here, in the climactic position at the end of the apocalyptic discourse, Mark places several verses which tell his readers how to live during the period in which they find themselves, between the resurrection and the parousia. These verses virtually cry out for allegorical interpretation as they speak about the situation

[19]O. J. Baab, "Father," *IDB* 2, 245.

[20]Ambrozic, *Hidden Kingdom*, 222-223, and Best, *Following*, 152.

in between the leaving and return of the master/lord (κύριος) of the house. During this interim period, his servants (δοῦλοι) are put in charge, each having an assigned task. There seems to be little question that the κύριος who has left and whose return is watched for is the risen Christ.[21] That Mark intends his readers to see the master's servants as allegorical representations of the disciples of Jesus is equally clear. It was pointed out above that Jesus has come "not to be served but to serve" (10:45) and that he calls upon his disciples to be servants/slaves of all (9:35-36; 10:43-44). It has also been suggested that there is a connection between the frequent references to "house" in Mark and the house-churches of early Christianity. This leads us to see the use of "house" in 13:34-35 as a reference to the community as the household of the Lord.[22] The emphasis on "watchfulness" (vss. 33, 35, 37), therefore, refers to Mark's own readers who live in between the departure of the Lord at the resurrection and his return at the parousia. This entire section of the apocalyptic discourse, in fact, suggests a community actively waiting for the return of the Lord.[23]

The Structure of the Community

Whenever one thinks about the structure of the early Christian community it is easy to read back into the New Testament texts the present situation in the church. If one is able to avoid this pitfall then the next potential stumbling block is the picture Luke provides us in his second volume. In Acts we find both horizontal and vertical differentiation occurring as the early church faces new situations and rapid expansion. Horizontal differentiation refers to the emergence

[21]See e.g., Nineham, *Saint Mark*, 361-362; Taylor, *St. Mark,* 523-524; and Achtemeier, *Invitation*, 190-191.

[22]P. S. Minear, *Commands of Christ* (Nashville: Abingdon, 1972) 156; Best, *Following*, 226-229; and Donahue, *Discipleship in Mark*, 31-32, 50-51.

[23]Ambrozic, *Hidden Kingdom*, 2, 222-223, and Donahue, *Discipleship in Mark*, 50-51.

of specialized and separate roles. There is a proliferation of roles and functions as mission personnel are commissioned to other cities, opponents need to be answered, and the new church needs to be interpreted to outsiders. Vertical differentiation designates the unequal power and influence attached to the various roles resulting in a status hierarchy. In Acts there is a rather clearly developed formal hierarchy of roles, titles, and authority.[24]

Our interest here, however, is neither in the structure of the church in the present age nor in the structure of the early community as it is portrayed in Acts. Once we recognize the importance of the communal dimension of Christian discipleship for Mark, we must examine his Gospel in an effort to see what it tells us about the structure of this early community.

What we find in Mark's Gospel is very little structural differentiation. Everyone seems to do everything without much status distinction. There is a functional distinction between Jesus and his followers, but very little evidence of functional specialization among these followers. The Twelve are singled out from among the larger group of disciples "to be with" Jesus "and to be sent out to preach and have authority to cast out demons" (3:14-15). But, as was seen above, others are "with" Jesus, preach, and cast out demons. Among the Twelve there is some rudimentary role specialization when Peter, James, and John (and sometimes Andrew) are singled out from among the larger group of Jesus' followers to witness the raising of Jairus' daughter (5:37) and the Transfiguration (9:2-9), to ask the question which leads to the apocalyptic discourse (13:3-4), and to go off with Jesus while he prays in Gethsemane (14:32ff.). Generally speaking, however, "the Twelve" and/or "the disciples" act together as a homogeneous unit, all of them able to perform the same functions.

The disciples of Jesus are seen debating their internal power and status on two occasions in Mark's Gospel (9:33-37; 10:41-45). In the first instance Jesus places a child in their midst and

[24]See D. B. Kraybill and D. M. Sweetland, "Possessions in Luke-Acts: A Sociological Perspective," *PRS* 10 (1983) 215-239.

talks to them about being servants of all. After the next argument, Jesus tells the disciples that the Gentiles exercise authority over each other but such activity is forbidden among them. In spite of this apparent prohibition against vertical differentiation, the prominent role of Peter in the Gospel[25] suggests that it always lurks beneath the surface.

Peter is the first one mentioned in the initial call story (1:16), his is the first name on the list of twelve (3:16-19), and he is the only member of the Twelve to have a relative healed (1:29-31). He is the first one of the Twelve who is given a new name (3:16), and when the inner group of disciples is named (Peter, James, John, and Andrew), Peter's name always appears first (5:37; 9:2; 13:3; 14:33). He is the only one whose denial Jesus predicts explicitly (14:29-31), and the only one whose denial Mark writes about in detail (14:66-72). In many instances Peter speaks for the group (8:27-33; 9:2-13; 10:28-30; 11:20-22), and he is the only disciple singled out by name when the young man dressed in white addresses the women at the empty tomb: "But go, tell his disciples and Peter that he is going before you to Galilee; there you will see him, as he told you" (16:7).

Does the prominence of Peter in Mark's Gospel mean that Mark has a hierarchical understanding of leadership in the Christian community? While this type of leadership certainly does develop in many early Christian communities, the evidence that Mark had this is mind is very weak. It is widely recognized that Mark paints a very complex picture of Peter. Although he is the first one called, his name is always listed first, and on numerous occasions he speaks for the group, he is also the only one whose denial is recorded in detail, the only one of the three Gethsemane sleepers singled out by name for a rebuke (14:37), and the only one whose opposition to Jesus is seen as satanic (8:33).

It is difficult to conclude that Peter is any better or any worse than the others who followed Jesus on his way. Peter

[25]R. E. Brown, et al, *Peter in the New Testament* (Minneapolis: Augsburg; New York: Paulist, 1973) 57-73, and Achtemeier *Mark*, 108f.

seems to embody both their strengths and their weaknesses. Because of this, and our earlier comments about the Twelve in general, it is likely that Mark sees Peter as a figure who is representative of the Twelve and, therefore, of all disciples. "Peter may also be the lesson *par excellence* for Christians as to the demands of discipleship upon them."[26]

On occasion someone will argue that the doorkeeper in the apocalyptic discourse (13:33-37) is meant to be seen as representing church leaders,[27] but such suggestions are unconvincing. Jesus' reference to the work given to each servant (vs. 34) and his statement that this teaching applies to all (vs. 37), indicates that the focus is not on the responsibility of the doorkeeper but on the obligations of all disciples.[28]

What is clear from the foregoing is that for Mark the disciple of Jesus is not a solitary individual, but a member of a community. When Jesus speaks about this community he uses familial language. His disciples are his new family, his brothers and sisters and mother (3:33-35). "Whoever does the will of God" (3:35) is considered a member of this new family of Jesus. Because the followers of Jesus are related to him in this way, they are also related to one another as brothers and sisters and mothers, members of the same family (10:28-31). In this new community there is no earthly father. This suggests that the community Mark has in mind is not hierarchical. Peter is singled out as an individual, and the Twelve are singled out as a group, yet Mark tells his story in such a way that Peter and the Twelve are best seen as symbolic representatives of the wider group, the disciples or the church. The egalitarian nature of the community is also seen in Jesus' words concerning how the Gentiles rule (10:42-45): "You know that those who are supposed to rule over the Gentiles lord it over them, and their great ones exercise authority over them. But it shall not be so among you." Instead of leadership

[26]Brown, *Peter*, 62. See also Achtemeier, *Mark*, 109.

[27]Minear, *Commands*, 156.

[28]Best, *Following*, 152-153; C. E. Carlston, *The Parables of the Triple Tradition* (Philadelphia: Fortress, 1975) 197-202; and Ambrozic *Hidden Kingdom*, 223.

and the exercise of authority, Jesus talks about service. He is not interested in telling Christian leaders how to behave, but in telling all disciples that the domination of others is contrary to his teaching about service. The requirement for the follower of Jesus is to help others rather than to control or dominate them.

The Community and the Kingdom

Our examination of Mark's Gospel has shown us that community is an important part of discipleship. What remains to be determined is whether or not membership in the Christian community is essential for salvation. What is the relationship between the church and the Kingdom of God?

Prior to C. H. Dodd's suggestion that ἤγγικεν (1:14-15) be translated as "has arrived" or "has come upon you," instead of "has come near,"[29] Jesus was thought to be announcing only the imminence of the Kingdom of God in Mark 1:14-15. Although scholarly opinion is still somewhat divided on this question, we believe that the best conclusion is that Jesus announced the arrival and present reality of the Kingdom of God.[30] Support for this position is found: (1) in the "parables of growth" (4:3-32) and (2) in verses which relate the Kingdom to "this present time" and the new community (10:15, 23-25, 29-30). Kelber has argued convincingly that Jesus' speech about the mystery of the Kingdom (4:3-32) reveals the reign of God as a present, even if unimpressive, reality.[31] The tension between the present and future dimensions of the Kingdom also is evident when Jesus says, "whoever does not receive the

[29] *The Parables of the Kingdom* (rev. ed. New York: Scribner's, 1961) 28-40, and "The Kingdom of God Has Come," *ExpTim* 48 (1936-37) 138-142.

[30] For an overview of the scholarly discussion see Ambrozic, *Hidden Kingdom*, 15ff., and Kelber, *Kingdom*, 7ff. Both these scholars argue for the present arrival of the Kingdom.

[31] *Kingdom*, 25-43.

Kingdom of God like a child shall not enter it" (10:15).[32] In addition, scholars believe that Mark conceives of the reign of God as present in 10:23-25[33] and 10:29-30.[34]

> [23]And Jesus looked around and said to his disciples, "How hard it is for those who have riches to enter the Kingdom of God!" [24]And the disciples were amazed at his words. But Jesus said to them again, "Children, how hard it is to enter the Kingdom of God! [25]It is easier for a camel to go through the eye of a needle than for a rich person to enter the Kingdom of God."

> [29]Jesus said, "Truly, I say to you, there is no one who has left house or brothers or sisters or mother or father or children or lands, for my sake and for the gospel, [30]who will not receive a hundredfold now in this time, houses and brothers and sisters and mothers and children and lands, with persecutions, and in the age to come eternal life."

In 10:29-30, there is a clear distinction made between what the disciple receives "in this time" and what the disciple will receive "in the age to come." The reward received in the present time by those who follow Jesus is quite clearly related to the life of the new community. The Kingdom will be revealed in its fullness only in the future, but Mark tells his readers that the reign of God came with Jesus and already exists in the present.

The Kingdom, which is made present in Jesus, should be (but is not *de facto*) made present in the community of disciples. This is clear when one realizes that Mark 1:15 is the context in which, and provides the reason for which, the disciples are called. Jesus invites those who hear him to be in and to work for the Kingdom. This is seen as well in the call to

---

[32]Taylor, *St. Mark*, 423; Schweizer, *Good News*, 207; and Ambrozic, *Hidden Kingdom*, 136-158.

[33]Taylor, *St. Mark*, 431, and Ambrozic, *Hidden Kingdom*, 158-171.

[34]Taylor, *St. Mark*, 434-435, and Ambrozic, *Hidden Kingdom*, 170.

be "with" Jesus, which Jesus issues to the Twelve as representatives of all disciples (3:14). The call to enter the Kingdom is equivalent to the call to be "with" Jesus, since Jesus is the Kingdom made present.

Mark believes that the Kingdom of God has come. Does this mean that he identifies it with the community of disciples, the church? Does membership in the church guarantee one's participation in the Kingdom of God? These questions must be addressed because there have been serious misunderstandings in the past. On the basis of Mark's Gospel it would be impossible to support either the traditional Protestant emphasis on the church as the "congregation of saints,"[35] or the pre-Vatican II conclusion by Catholics that the church and the Kingdom of God are identical.[36]

The easiest way to dispel the notion that membership in the community of disciples guarantees salvation is to point to Judas Iscariot. Although he is one of the Twelve whom Jesus appointed "to be with him, and to be sent out to preach and to have authority to cast out demons" (3:14-15, 19), he is the one who betrays Jesus into the hands of the Jewish authorities (14:10-11, 17-21, 43ff.). Two prominent biblical scholars who have studied what Mark has to say concerning the Kingdom of God, Werner H. Kelber, a Lutheran, and Aloysius M. Ambrozic, a Catholic, agree that even though the Kingdom is present, repentance and faith are still necessary. Because of the hidden nature of the Kingdom in the present it is still possible for members of the Christian community to fail to do the will of God.[37]

---

[35]See e.g., W. Pannenberg, *Theology and the Kingdom of God* (Philadelphia: Westminster, 1969) 75ff., and C.E. Braaten, *The Future of God* (New York: Harper & Row, 1969) 133. Both Lutheran scholars argue that Protestantism has focused too much on the piety and salvation of church members themselves.

[36]That the nature and mission of the church are to be understood in relationship to and in subordination to the Kingdom of God is seen in Vatican II's *Dogmatic Constitution on the Church*, 5 and *Pastoral Constitution on the Church in the Modern World*, 45. This is also the position of modern Catholic scholars such as K. Rahner, "Church and World," *Encyclopedia of Theology* (New York: Seabury, 1975) 239, and Lohfink, *Jesus and Community*, 64, 70.

[37]Kelber, *Kingdom*, 14, and Ambrozic, *Hidden Kingdom,* 135ff.

Markan scholars generally agree: (1) that the Kingdom of God is present and active in the church and the world, and (2) that it is neither a visible reality nor subject to earthly developments as is the church.[38] The obvious conclusion, therefore, is that the Kingdom and the church are not identical according to Mark. The church is an imperfect and incomplete embodiment of the Kingdom, because it is an imperfect and incomplete embodiment of Christ's continued presence.

The conclusion that, according to Mark, membership in the Christian community does not guarantee one's salvation leaves us with one more question to answer: Is salvation, being included in the Kingdom of God, impossible for one who is outside the community of Jesus' disciples?

Although Mark neither raises nor deals directly with this question, in order to understand his teaching on community it is important for us to suggest how he might have answered it. (1) Because, as is widely agreed, the Gospel was written by a believer, for believers, thus far we have been discussing how one becomes a disciple of Jesus and what is expected of the person who is called to follow Jesus. What we must be aware of, however, is that "Jesus never specified membership in the circle of disciples as a condition for entering the kingdom of God."[39] (2) After his exchange with the rich man, Jesus responds to the disciples' question, "Then who can be saved?" (10:26) by saying "all things are possible with God" (10:27). This reaffirms the absolute gratuity of salvation and shows that even the failure to respond to a discipleship summons does not preclude salvation.[40] (3) In the universal moral directive discussed earlier, Jesus states that "whoever does the will of God" (3:35) is a member of his eschatological family. (4) When his disciples want to silence the exorcist, who was not a member of their little band, Jesus responds, "Do not

---

[38]Ambrozic, *Hidden Kingdom*, 102, 133, and R. Schnackenburg, *Das Evangelium nach Markus* (Düsseldorf: Patmos, 1966) 117.

[39]Lohfink, *Jesus and Community*, 34.

[40]Donahue, *Discipleship in Mark*, 40.

forbid him; for no one who does a mighty work in my name will be able soon after to speak evil of me. For he that is not against us is for us" (9:39-40). In light of the above, the best conclusion is that doing the will of God, which may or may not involve becoming a Christian, is the requirement for salvation. What is important is that one seek and do the will of God. "Mark's gospel, therefore, is directed to those who have been converted and believe in the gospel (1:15) but also reaches out to those who may be seeking the way of God in truth and therefore are not far from the kingdom of God."[41]

Conclusion

Those who are called by Jesus to be his followers must develop both a deep personal relationship with him and an intense concern for the well-being of others. They must proclaim the good news by the example of their own lives and their active application of Gospel values in their struggle to insure social justice, peace, and human rights. Part of the good news is that the Christian disciple is not called to undertake this arduous task alone. The call to discipleship includes with it a call to become a member of a new community. Here, within the family of Jesus, one finds the sustenance, support, and love, that usually characterize the relationships among members of the same biological family. What is missing from this community is a father who has virtually absolute power over the other members of the family. Instead of this typical first-century family model, we find an egalitarian community whose members encourage and assist one another as they actively involve themselves in serving all.

As important as membership in the visible community of disciples is for one who is called to acknowledge the Lordship of Jesus, it does not by itself guarantee salvation. What is necessary for salvation is membership in the Kingdom of God

---

[41] Donahue, "A Neglected Factor," 594.

which: (1) exists within the community but is not identical with it and (2) should be made visible in the lives of the disciples. For those who have not been called to acknowledge the Lordship of Jesus and who are not members of the visible community of disciples, salvation is still possible. Whoever does the will of God is a member of the Kingdom. One should be very cautious when it comes to the issue of who will be saved, for as Jesus tells us, "All things are possible with God" (10:27).

6

Life Within the Community

In this chapter we will take a closer look at the Christian community we began to discuss in our previous chapter. After pointing out (1) that the community is inclusive and not exclusive, we will look at what Mark has to say about: (2) Eucharist and Baptism, (3) Marriage, Children and Possessions, and (4) Prayer.

United and Inclusive

The fact that Jesus continually travels back and forth across the Sea of Galilee, in Mark 4:35–8:21, has interested readers of Mark's Gospel for many years. It was mentioned earlier that Mark does not present Jesus as an aimless wanderer in his Gospel, but as someone with a definite direction, purpose, and goal. What does Mark want his readers to understand about Jesus and his message in this section of the Gospel with its numerous crossings of the Sea of Galilee?

Trained and untrained readers alike also want to know why Mark has included two stories about Jesus feeding the multitudes (6:30-44; 8:1-10). These stories seem to be rather important since: (1) After each multiplication story, the reader is informed that the disciples failed to understand about the loaves; and, (2) Jesus summarizes his entire northern ministry by asking his disciples to recall specific details from the two feeding stories.

Immediately following the feeding of the 5,000, Jesus makes his disciples get into a boat and go before him to the other side of the lake. The disciples appear to be making little headway and are experiencing great distress rowing against the wind. When Jesus sees this he begins walking toward them on the sea. Eventually he joins them in the boat at which time the wind ceases. Mark then informs us that "they were utterly astounded for they did not understand about the loaves" (6:51b-52a). What is it that they do not understand?

Shortly after the second feeding story, in which 4,000 were fed, Jesus and his disciples again set out in a boat to cross the Sea of Galilee. Jesus chooses this time, at the end of his northern ministry, to castigate his followers for their lack of comprehension and to offer them some hints which, one assumes, should lead them to a proper understanding of his ministry thus far:

> **8** [18b]And do you not remember? [19]When I broke the five loaves for the five thousand, how many baskets full of broken pieces did you take up?" They said to him, "Twelve." [20]"And the seven for the four thousand, how many baskets full of broken pieces did you take up?" And they said to him, "Seven." [21]And he said to them, "Do you not yet understand?"

The question, of course, is the same one that was mentioned above: what is it that Jesus wants them to understand?

There are several possible answers to this question,[1] but the one which interests us most at the moment is the suggestion

---

[1]As was pointed out earlier, these words of Jesus are followed immediately by the first blind man story and the central section of the Gospel, in which Jesus teaches his disciples about the necessity of his suffering and death. See Quesnell, *Mind of Mark*, 257-260, who concludes that there are seven possible meanings expressed simultaneously in 6:52.

that Mark has used the travels of Jesus around Gaililee and its environs to reflect symbolically the unity of Jew (west of the Sea of Galilee) and Gentile (east of the Sea and northwards) in the new community.[2] The fact that the two feeding stories take place on opposite sides of the Sea of Galilee suggests that perhaps Mark sees Jesus as a great unifier in this section of the Gospel, someone who is inaugurating the Kingdom of God on the Gentile side of the lake as well as on the Jewish side of the lake.[3]

The probability that this suggestion is accurate increases as one notices the other similarities between what happens on the western side and on the eastern side of the Sea of Galilee. The first miracle that Jesus performs in the Gospel is the exorcism in Capernaum (1:21-28), on the Jewish side of the lake. This is immediately followed by his next miracle, the healing of Peter's mother-in-law (1:29-31). The same pattern, exorcism followed by healing, takes place on the eastern or Gentile side of the lake. Jesus crosses the lake for the first time after his Kingdom speech in chapter 4. The storm is stilled and Jesus and his disciples arrive at the country of the Gerasenes. It is here that Jesus performs his most massive exorcism in Mark as he casts out the unclean spirits from the Gerasene demoniac (5:1-20). After performing this exorcism, Jesus returns to the Jewish side of the lake where, among other things, he raises Jairus' daughter and cures the woman who has been hemorrhaging. The story of Jesus' return trip to the Gentile side of the lake begins in 6:45 where once again, as on the first trip, we see him calming the wind (6:45-52). After Jesus and his disciples arrive at Gennesaret he begins to heal the sick people who are brought to him (6:53-56), as he had healed Peter's mother-in-law. Thus, the same pattern we saw

[2]Kelber, *Kingdom*, 48ff. See also N. A. Beck, "Reclaiming a Biblical Text: The Mark 8:14-21 Discussion about Bread in the Boat," *CBQ* 43 (1981) 49-56.

[3]See Nineham, *Saint Mark*, 207-208, who points out that "it was suggested at least as early as the fourth century that St. Mark may have intended the feeding of the five thousand to symbolize the giving of the Bread of Life to the Jews, and the feeding of the four thousand the giving of the Bread of Life to the Gentiles."

on the Jewish side of the lake, exorcism followed by healing, takes place on the Gentile side of the lake.

There is also a similarity in what Mark reports immediately following each exorcism, Jesus' first miracle on each side of the lake. After the Capernaum exorcism Mark tells us that Jesus' "fame spread everywhere throughout all the surrounding region of Galilee" (1:28). Similarly, after the exorcism in the country of the Gerasenes, Mark tells us that the healed man "went away and began to proclaim in the Decapolis how much Jesus had done for him; and all the people marveled" (5:20). Thus, the good news is proclaimed to those in the Decapolis as it was earlier to those in Galilee. First to the Jews, then to the Gentiles, just as Jesus himself indicates in the story of the Syrophoenician woman:

> 7 27And he said to her, "Let the children first be fed, for it is not right to take the children's bread and throw it to the dogs."

This story of Jesus' encounter with the Syrophoenician woman contributes to the unity motif. There is an obvious connection between the bread saying of 7:27 and the two feeding miracles. (1) In Mark's Gospel, the verb $\chi o \rho \tau \acute{a} \zeta \epsilon \iota \nu$ (to feed/satisfy) occurs only in 7:27 and in the two feeding pericopes (6:42; 8:4, 8). (2) Jesus' comment, "Let the children first be fed" (7:27), has already been fulfilled in the Feeding of the 5,000. Thus, the way is prepared for the second feeding story. (3) Much of the material between the first feeding passage and the story of the Syrophoenician woman has to do with Jewish eating customs. These pericopes, which treat ritual washing (7:1-8) and dietary laws (7:14-23), move from an exclusive to an inclusive perception of community.

The role that Jesus and his disciples play in each of the lake crossings points toward the unification theme as well. The first time they go to the Gentile side of the lake (4:35-41) it is Jesus who leads the way. The disciples misunderstand, however, seeing the stilling of the storm only as a dramatic nature miracle; the real significance of the trip across the lake

eludes them.[4] The disciples fail to see that Jesus is breaking
down the barrier to the Gentiles. The message is that both
Jews and Gentiles can become members of the Kingdom of
God and the new community of Jesus. The disciples should
have understood this, as is clear from the role they are
expected to play in the second crossing (6:45-52). The second
time they all travel across the Sea of Galilee Jesus makes his
disciples go before him. He has shown them the way earlier;
now it is up to them to conduct the mission to the Gentiles.
Supporting this reading is the fact that Jesus feeds the 4,000
because they have been with him for three days (8:2). Just as
Jesus took pity on the Gentiles after three days, so his
disciples will begin the mission to the Gentiles after the death
and resurrection of Jesus.[5]

In the feeding stories themselves there are indications that
Mark is referring to the unification of Jew and Gentile in the
community and in the Kingdom of God, the very thing that
the disciples should have learned during the northern ministry
of Jesus. After the feeding of the 5,000, on the Jewish side of
the lake, the disciples gathered twelve baskets of leftovers
(6:43). Seven baskets of fragments were collected after the
feeding on the Gentile side of the lake (8:8). The fact that there
were twelve tribes of Israel suggests that the number twelve,
appearing as it does in 6:43 and 8:19, should be seen as
representing the Jews.[6] Although the number seven is not
specifically a Gentile number,[7] in the ancient world it does
denote completeness, perfection, and consummation.[8] If
Mark has the unity motif in mind here, as we have claimed,
then the use of the number seven, meaning wholeness or

---

[4]Kelber, *Kingdom*, 50, 58.

[5]Ibid., 61.

[6]See Nineham, *Saint Mark*, 207.

[7]The only hint that seven might be a symbolic representation of the Gentiles
appears in Acts where the group of Hellenists appointed to assist the Twelve (Acts
6:1-6) number seven and are referred to as "the seven" (Acts 21:8).

[8]M. H. Pope, "Seven, Seventh, Seventy," *IDB* 4, 294-295.

completeness, would be appropriate.[9] The great miracle of Jesus, therefore, is not his quieting of the storms but his inclusion of the Gentiles in the Kingdom of God.

There is one more reference to bread which also conveys the idea of Jesus as a unifier. In the pericope which summarizes and ends the northern ministry of Jesus (8:13-21) Mark tells us that the disciples had "forgotten to bring bread" (8:14a) and Jesus asks them, "Why do you discuss the fact that you have no bread?" (8:17). In between these verses about there being no bread, we learn that the disciples did in fact have some bread with them, albeit "only one loaf" (8:14b). While one should be cautious in reading too much into this, it is true that Jesus is referred to as the Bread of Life in John's Gospel (6:35ff.). Perhaps Mark intends his readers to see Jesus as the one loaf that is in the boat with the disciples.[10]

The obvious conclusion to the foregoing is that the disciples of Jesus, by being with him during his northern ministry, should have learned that there is no distinction between Jew or Gentile in the Kingdom of God. Because Jesus himself is presented as a unifier and because it is reasonable to assume that the community is trying to live in accordance with the teachings and example of Jesus, there should be no such racial or ethnic discrimination in the Christian community.

Although it is Paul who is remembered for saying that "there is neither Jew nor Greek, there is neither slave nor free, there is neither male nor female; for you are all one in Christ

[9]Mark's interest in numbers has been widely recognized. Commonly noted are: (1) The Transfiguration, which takes place "after six days" (9:2), has many affinities with Moses coming out of the mist on Mount Sinai "on the seventh day" because the cloud had covered it for "six days" (Ex. 24:16-18). (2) There are five controversy stories (2:1-3:6) and five parts to the Kingdom of God speech (4:13-32). (3) There are three disciples who are singled out from the rest (3:16-17; 5:37; 9:2; 14:32), three failures and three successes in the parable of the Sower (4:15-20), three passion-resurrection predictions (8:31; 9:31; 10:33-34), three times that Jesus separates from his disciples to pray in Gethsemane (14:32-42), and three denials by Peter (14:66-72).

[10]Quesnell, *Mind of Mark*, 242-243. See also Kelber, *Kingdom*, 58, 61, and Beck, "Reclaiming," 54ff., who argues that in the pre-Markan tradition this pericope stressed the importance of uniting Jews and Gentiles "into open-table fellowship where one loaf would be sufficient."

Jesus" (Gal. 3:28), Mark seems to agree with him. We have just seen how Mark has told a Gospel story in such a way that his readers are led to understand that in the Kingdom of God, and therefore in any genuine Christian community, there is no racial discrimination. In addition to this stress on the unity of Jew and Gentile, there is also a "noticeable pattern of sexual parallelism"[11] in Mark 4:35–8:21. Jesus shows concern first for a man (the Geresene demoniac), then for two women (Jairus' daughter and the hemorrhaging woman), for two more women (the Syrophoenician woman and her daughter), and finally for another man (the deaf mute). When one combines this with the fact, discussed above, that many women followed Jesus and fulfilled the Markan requirement for discipleship as they obeyed Jesus' call to service (15:41), it is clear that in the Kingdom of God there is no sexual discrimination. Our comments above on the egalitarian nature of the Christian community pictured in Mark point unmistakably to the conclusion that, as far as Mark is concerned, there ought to be "neither male nor female" in the community of disciples.

The Christian community, according to Mark, is united and pursuing unity. In his Gospel Mark presents Jesus as a unifier who breaks through ethnic and sexual barriers to present the good news to all. Through word and deed Jesus demonstrates that the Kingdom of God is open to women as well as men and Gentiles as well as Jews. Those who do the will of God are already united as members of the still hidden Kingdom. Those who have been called to follow Jesus as his disciples have also been called to membership in his community on earth. As members of this visible community, the church, they are called to become what they already are, united as brothers, sisters, and mothers of one another and of Jesus, children of God.

[11]Kelber, *Kingdom*, 61.

Eucharist and Baptism

EUCHARIST

It was mentioned above that there are several possible ways in which Mark might be using the two feeding stories he includes in his Gospel. In addition to the unity motif, there are a number of scholars who believe that there is a Eucharistic theme associated with these pericopes.[12] Proponents of this position point out: (1) The same sequence of taking, blessing, breaking, and distributing to the disciples appears in the feeding stories (6:41; 8:6) and in the Last Supper (14:22). (2) Mark's use of εὐχαριστεῖν (to give thanks) in the second feeding story (8:6) is similar to Paul's use of the same verb in his description of the Eucharist in 1 Corinthians 11:24. (3) Matthew and Luke reduce the importance of the fish motif, thus emphasizing the parallelism between the feedings and the Eucharist. (4) In John's Gospel, which contains a sequence of events similar to those in Mark, we find a discourse on the Eucharist following directly after the feeding story (6:35-58).[13]

A close reading of Mark's first feeding story as it now stands (6:32-44) reveals that Jesus does not take pity on the crowd because they are hungry, but because they are "like sheep without a shepherd" (6:34). Within the context of Mark's Gospel this points to a time after the death of Jesus. In his speech on the Mount of Olives (14:27) Jesus interprets Zechariah 13:7, "I will strike the shepherd, and the sheep will be scattered," as referring to his own imminent death and the scattering of his disciples (14:50). Thus, because of Mark's editorial activity in 6:34 (a widely accepted fact), the focus of the feeding of the 5,000 is on the future, after the death of

[12]See especially Quesnell, *Mind of Mark*, who argues that Mark believes Christ crucified and risen is present in the Eucharistic worship of the church, and J.-M. Van Cangh, *La Multiplication des pains et l'Eucharistie* (Paris: Cerf, 1975).

[13]See P. J. Achtemeier, "The Origin and Function of the Pre-Marcan Miracle Catenae," *JBL* 91 (1972) 198-221, who depends in part on B. van Iersel, "Die wunderbare Speisung und das Abendmahl in der synoptischen Tradition," *NovT* 7 (1964) 167-194.

Jesus when the community will be leaderless.[14] This is similar to the focus of the feeding of the 4,000 which, as was discussed above, is on the Gentile mission that takes place after the death and resurrection of Jesus.

It seems likely that these two feeding stories were understood as referring to the Eucharist in the pre-Markan tradition.[15] Mark does not ignore or downplay this Eucharistic dimension but, by introducing verses which refer to the death of Jesus (6:34; 8:2),[16] he reinterprets it. The emphasis on the miraculous aspect of the feeding stories, the divine power of Jesus, is reinterpreted in light of the characteristic Markan stress on the death of Jesus.[17]

If Achtemeier is correct, the tradition Mark inherited called attention to the powerful presence of Christ himself at the Eucharistic celebration, but said little or nothing about his death.[18] While Mark does not wish to deny either the power or presence of the risen Lord, he realizes that this is an unacceptable interpretation of the Eucharist and its origins. The Eucharist should not be understood exclusively in terms of the glorified Christ and the Eucharistic celebration should not be seen as grounded only in the powerful feeding miracles of Jesus' earthly career. As far as Mark is concerned, the Eucharist calls attention to the suffering and death of Jesus

[14]It is possible to argue that the strong resurrection motif in the Walking on the Water story (6:45-52) forms the second half of this diptych: $\phi\acute{a}\nu\tau a\sigma\mu a$ ("ghost"; cf. Luke 24:37D), '$\epsilon\gamma\acute{\omega}$ $\epsilon\acute{\iota}'\mu\iota$ ("it is I"; cf. Luke 24:39), $\mu\grave{\eta}$ $\phi o\beta\epsilon\widehat{\iota}\sigma\theta\epsilon$ ("fear not"; cf. Matthew 28:10).

[15]See Achtemeier, "Origin and Function," 207f., who argues that Mark is not responsible for the Eucharistic overtones in the two feeding stories. Cf. Beck, "Reclaiming," 51-56; R. M. Fowler, *Loaves and Fishes* (SBLDS 54; Ann Arbor: Edwards Brothers, 1981) 83-84; and J. A. Grassi, "The Eucharist in the Gospel of Mark," *AER* 168 (1974) 595-608.

[16]There is widespread agreement that both verses are products of Markan editorial activity.

[17]See V. K. Robbins, "Last Meal: Preparation, Betrayal, and Absence (Mark 14:12-25)," in *Passion*, 21-40.

[18]Achtemeier, "Origin and Function," 213ff.

prior to his glorification and is grounded in the Last Supper.[19] This is clear from the context in which Mark locates the words of institution (14:17-31),[20] and the placement of the first feeding story.

As it now stands, we find the Eucharistic institution (14:22-25) surrounded by verses which deal with betrayal, abandonment, and denial. Immediately preceding the words about the bread and the cup, Jesus speaks about the betrayer:

> **14** [18]"Truly, I say to you, one of you will betray me, one who is eating with me." [19]They began to be sorrowful, and to say to him one after another, "Is it I?" [20]He said to them, "It is one of the Twelve, one who is dipping bread in the same dish with me. [21]For the Son of Man goes as it is written of him, but woe to that man by whom the Son of Man is betrayed! It would have been better for that man if he had not been born."

After the words of institution Jesus, now on the Mount of Olives, says to his disciples:

> **14** [27]"You will all fall away; for it is written, 'I will strike the shepherd, and the sheep will be scattered.' [28]But after I am raised up, I will go before you to Galilee." [29]Peter said to him, "Even though they all fall away, I will not." [30]And Jesus said to him, "Truly, I say to you, this very night, before the cock crows twice, you will deny me three times." [31]But he said vehemently, "If I must die with you, I will not deny you." And they all said the same.

[19]Mark is not the first New Testament writer to emphasize this (cf. 1 Corinthians 10:16-17; 11:23-26).

[20]This position would be even more certain if W. Marxsen, *The Lord's Supper as a Christological Problem* (trans. L. Nieting; Philadelphia: Fortress, 1970) 17-18, is correct and Mark has inserted 14:22-25 into a passion narrative that did not mention the Eucharistic institution.

The same connection between the Eucharist and the suffering and death of Jesus can be seen in Mark 6.

6:7-13	Mission of the Twelve
6:14-29	Death of John the Baptist
6:30-33	Return of Those Who Were Sent
6:34-44	Feeding of the Five Thousand

By placing the Feeding of the 5,000 immediately after the "sandwich" of the mission of the disciples, which encloses the story of the death of John the Baptist, Mark has drawn attention to the suffering and death of John which foreshadow the passion and death of Jesus. For Mark, therefore, the Eucharist is based not on the miraculous deeds of Jesus but on his sacrifice on the cross.

The motif of discipleship as service can also be found in the feeding stories. The disciples' effort to send the crowds away (6:35-36) is countered by Jesus' command, "You give them something to eat" (6:37). In both pericopes the disciples actively participate in the feeding of the multitudes (6:41; 8:6-7). Their failure to understand, apparent within the feeding stories themselves (6:37; 8:4), remains after they serve the crowds however (8:14-21). In the central section of the Gospel, which follows immediately after Jesus highlights the disciples' misunderstanding, Mark emphasizes that discipleship involves service.

It is time for us to restate the question asked above: What is it that the disciples of Jesus are supposed to understand when he asks them (8:17-21) to recall the number of baskets of fragments they gathered after the two feeding stories? We have already concluded that the disciples are expected to understand that Jesus is a unifier whose two feeding miracles symbolically reflect the unity of Jew and Gentile in the new community.[21] Now we can add that Mark also believes the

---

[21]There also seems to be an eschatological dimension here as the abundance of food suggests the eschatological banquet in the Kingdom.

disciples should understand the relationship between the Eucharist and the suffering and death of Jesus. As we have seen previously, the focus in Mark's Gospel is on the cross and not on power and glory. What the disciples continually fail to understand is that following Jesus does not mean having miraculous power and authority; instead it means taking up your cross and following Jesus in the way of the cross.

BAPTISM

There is virtually unanimous agreement that just as there never was a time in the life of the church when there was no Eucharist, there never was a time in the life of the church when there was no baptism. The roots of this ancient practice, Christian baptism, are usually seen to lie in the ministry of John the Baptist. Although the origin of the water baptism practiced by John and other Jewish sects and groups is much debated, the most likely background is Jewish proselyte (convert) baptism. John's startling innovation with respect to this Jewish practice was "that such an act was necessary for Jews. John was thereby treating them just like pagans."[22]

Mark introduces Jesus to us in his first chapter (1:19) as one who "came from Nazareth of Galilee and was baptized by John in the Jordan." John, as the reader has just learned, is "preaching a baptism of repentance for the forgiveness of sins" (1:4). Many have availed themselves of the opportunity to be baptized by John (1:5) and one mightier than John is coming who will baptize with the Holy Spirit (1:8).

Baptism is a major topic in the first nine verses of Mark's Gospel, but it does not dominate the Gospel as a whole. Two-thirds of the Markan usages of $\beta\alpha\pi\tau\acute{\iota}\zeta\epsilon\iota\nu$ (to baptize) are in Mark 1:4-9.[23] Neither Jesus nor his disciples baptize in this Gospel. Jesus does appoint the Twelve to preach and cast out demons, but no mention is made of baptizing anyone.

---

[22]Reumann, *Jesus,* 317f.

[23]The use of $\beta\alpha\pi\tau\acute{\iota}\zeta\epsilon\iota\nu$ in 7:4 as ceremonial dipping or washing need not concern us. The only other uses of this verb are in 10:38, 39 and will be examined below.

Similarly, when Jesus sends the Twelve on their mission he talks about healing, exorcizing, and preaching repentance (6:7-13), but not about baptizing. Although most treatments of Christian baptism discuss the death-resurrection motif, the theme of initiation, and the notion of admission to a new community, none of these themes is present in Mark 1. The wider theological answer is that Christian baptism, a baptism "with the Holy Spirit"(1:8), was possible only after Pentecost, when the Spirit was given. It is reasonable to conclude that Mark agrees with this and that this is the reason neither Jesus nor his disciples are presented as baptizing in Mark's Gospel.

The fact remains, however, that Jesus himself was baptized by John (1:9-11). The impression one gets from these verses is that Jesus approves this "baptism of repentance for the forgiveness of sins"(1:4). It does not follow that Mark intends to present Jesus as a sinner. Mark has informed his readers that Jesus is the Son of God (1:1) and that God is well pleased with him (1:11). The usual theological answer to this problem is to conclude that Jesus is identifying himself completely with the sinful people of Israel.

It is not enough simply to say that Mark's readers would have been familiar with Christian baptism. We are interested in what the Gospel of Mark itself says about this rite. Thus far we have concluded that Jesus approves of the baptism of John which involved repentance and was required of all. What we will examine now are those verses in which Mark connects baptism with the death of Jesus.

Just as Mark saw a relationship between the Eucharist and the suffering and death of Jesus, so he sees a relationship between baptism and the suffering and death of Jesus. Two of the three times Mark uses $\beta \alpha \pi \tau i \zeta \epsilon \iota \nu$ outside his first chapter occur in Jesus' third discipleship discourse, examined earlier. After the third passion-resurrection prediction, James and John ask Jesus for positions of power and prestige in the Kingdom. Jesus responds by saying: "You do not know what you are asking. Are you able to drink the cup that I drink, or to be baptized with the baptism with which I am baptized?" (10:38). The brothers tell Jesus that they are able to do this and Jesus says, "The cup that I drink you will drink; and with the baptism with which I am baptized, you will be baptized" (10:39).

Elsewhere in the New Testament we read that Christian baptism incorporates one into the death, burial, and resurrection of Jesus, into "life with him" (Col. 2:12; Eph. 2:1, 4-6; Phil. 3:10-11). Baptism purifies (Eph. 5:26) as we become "dead to sin but alive for God in Christ Jesus" (Rom. 6:11). Mark is not the only New Testament author, therefore, who locates the meaning of baptism in Jesus' death.

If one focuses only on the effects of baptism on the individual it is likely that theological individualism, discussed earlier, will once again appear. Those Christians who concentrate only on the cleansing effects of baptism and the reception of the Holy Spirit risk distorting the Christian understanding of baptism. Mark's theology of baptism answers any such tendency to focus exclusively on the power of the Holy Spirit and the freedom from one's sins. (1) Mark reminds us that baptism includes μετάνοια (1:4). As we discussed earlier, μετάνοια (repentance) involves a radical conversion from all that is evil and a total commitment to God. It includes the obligation to strive to live a holy life.[24] (2) Mark places references to baptism in 10:38-39 which clearly and unambiguously connect baptism with the suffering and death of Jesus. In addition to what has been already mentioned, the two uses of ποτήριον (cup) in these verses serve to connect Mark's teaching on baptism with his Eucharistic theology (14:23) and to connect both with the agony of Jesus in Gethsemane (14:36)[25] Once again readers of Mark's Gospel are told of the centrality of the cross in understanding Jesus and what it means to follow him.

---

[24]See D. J. Murray, "Mark's Theology of Baptism," *Dimension* 8 (1976) 92-97.

[25]Other than the four uses of ποτήριον already mentioned (10:38, 39; 14:23, 36) Mark only uses this word in 7:4 and 9:41.

Marriage, Children, and Possessions

MARRIAGE

Jesus' teaching on marriage (10:1-12) is found in the central section of Mark's Gospel, between the second and third predictions of his passion-resurrection. Scholars often puzzle over why Mark has included this pericope at this particular point in the Gospel, since it seems at first glance to have little in common with what precedes it.[26] Further investigation, however, discloses that these verses are probably part of a larger pre-Markan unit (10:1-31) that deals with marriage, children, and possessions.[27] Mark would have included these verses at this point because, just as in chapter 9, Jesus is shown teaching his disciples about the character and cost of discipleship.[28]

As Jesus begins his southern ministry (10:1), he is confronted by some Pharisees who ask him a question about whether or not it is lawful for a man to divorce his wife (10:2). This is a peculiar question on the lips of a Pharisee, since Deuteronomy 24:1-4 clearly allows a husband to divorce his wife (although the wife could not divorce her husband). In first-century Judaism the dispute was not about the right to divorce, but about what constituted valid reasons for divorce. The crucial text is Deuteronomy 24:1: "When a man takes a wife and marries her, if then she finds no favor in his eyes because he has found some indecency in her" he may write her a bill of divorce, put it in her hand, and send her out of his house. Some concluded that this verse allowed for divorce only for the most serious causes (e.g., adultery), while others

[26]Quesnell, *Mind of Mark*, 150ff.; Best, *Following*, 100; and Nineham, *Saint Mark*, 259f.

[27]J. Jeremias, *Infant Baptism in the First Four Centuries* (trans. D. Cairns; Philadelphia: Westminster, 1960) 50. See also Best, *Following*, 99, 102 n.4, and Achtemeier, *Invitation*, 143ff.

[28]It is also possible that the threefold use of παιδίον (child) in 10:13-15 (the last three uses of this word in the Gospel) influenced Mark's placement of this section in close proximity to 9:36-37, where παιδίον appears twice.

read this verse as permitting divorce for virtually any reason at all.

In its present context, Mark apparently sees the Pharisees as either testing Jesus' knowledge of the law or testing whether he will set himself against the law of Moses. Regardless of what Mark believes motivated the question, Jesus demonstrates in his answer that he is familiar with the Deuteronomy text, yet believes that two other texts from the Torah take precedence (Gen. 1:27; 2:24).

> **10** 5Jesus said to them, "For your hardness of heart he [Moses] wrote you this commandment. 6But from the beginning of creation, 'God made them male and female.' 7'For this reason a man shall leave his father and mother and be joined to his wife, 8and the two shall become one.' So they are no longer two but one. 9What therefore God has joined together, let not human beings put asunder."

Although Moses allowed divorce as a concession to human sinfulness ("hardness of heart"), Jesus points out that this is contrary to the will of God in creating the human race.

The importance of this teaching is highlighted in verses 10-12 where the original saying of Jesus is extended to cover both sexes.

> 10And in the house the disciples asked him again about this matter. 11And he said to them, "Whoever divorces his wife and marries another commits adultery against her; 12and if she divorces her husband and marries another, she commits adultery."

Although verses 11-12 make the same point as verses 2-9, in effect they extend the teaching of Jesus beyond its original Jewish setting into the wider Greco-Roman world. A woman had the right to initiate a divorce (10:12) under Roman law, but not according to Jewish legal custom. These verses show that as the early Christian community encountered the Roman legal situation, it adapted this saying about marriage in order to preserve its original intention.[29] According to Mark, Jesus teaches that marriage is willed by God, and that both husband and wife must understand the importance of maintaining the marriage bond intact.

This would have been a difficult message for many to bear in the sexually permissive Roman society. The would-be Christian is being told that the cost of discipleship includes adopting a new sexual ethic, one which goes against the accepted values of the wider society. Some have gone so far as to call this taking up one's cross and denying oneself.[30] While this may be how the text was intended to be read, there is at least one other possibility worth mentioning. In our examination of Mark's Gospel thus far, we have stressed several times that the one who would follow Jesus as his disciple must leave all behind. This "all" was defined as family, friends, occupation, and possessions. It is likely that the early Christians asked whether or not the marriage bond could be or had to be dissolved on behalf of the new community. As one rereads the texts mentioned earlier one notices that the marriage relationship is singled out as the one exception to the requirement of separation and divorce in the message of Jesus. Nowhere in Mark is it mentioned that a male disciple has permanently left his wife to follow Jesus, and nowhere is it stated that a female follower of Jesus has permanently left her husband in order to join Jesus on his way. This conclusion about the indissolubility of the marriage bond is strengthened by Jesus' words concerning his new family (10:29-30). As was mentioned above, neither husband nor wife are included among what must be renounced for Jesus' sake and for the gospel (10:29).

According to Mark 10:2-12, Jesus believed that the marriage bond was permanent and that husband and wife were equal within the marriage relationship. These teachings

[29]Because this extension is also implied by Paul in 1 Corinthians 7:10-11, Mark may not be responsible for its introduction here. See H. C. Kee, *Community Of The New Age* (Philadelphia: Westminster, 1977) 155, however, who argues that Mark is unmistakably responsible for the addition of these verses.

[30]Best, *Following*, 100-101.

set Jesus and his followers apart from both the Jewish and pagan worlds in which they lived. One should be cautious, however, about making wide-ranging claims concerning marriage and divorce in the modern world based on the foregoing. (1) In order to come to any conclusion about the New Testament teaching on marriage and divorce, several other texts would have to be examined, including the famous "divorce exception clause" (Mt. 5:32; 19:9). (2) One would have to address the position of some scholars that if Mark 10:2-12 is read as legislation it would go against the trend of Jesus' teaching as a whole which is against legalism.[31] (3) The Pharisees ask what is allowed (10:2, 4), but Jesus responds in terms of what God has commanded (10:3, 7). Therefore, one would have to consider the suggestion that these verses express the absolute will of God in this matter, but do not discuss what is to be done if human sinfulness ("hardness of heart") persists.[32]

Whether or not one believes that Jesus is legislating a rule on divorce here, it is widely agreed that in Mark 10:2-12 Jesus is proclaiming the sanctity of marriage.

CHILDREN

Jesus' words on marriage and divorce are followed immediately by a pericope dealing with children. Earlier we saw that one who received a child in Jesus' name received both Jesus and the one who sent him (9:36-37). The present verses inform us that anyone who wishes to enter the Kingdom of God must receive the Kingdom like a child (10:15).[33]

---

[31]Taylor, *St. Mark*, 421, and Nineham, *Saint Mark*, 265. See also W. Kasper, *Theology of Christian Marriage* (trans. D. Smith; New York; Crossroad, 1983) 51, 70.

[32]Achtemeier, *Invitation*, 144.

[33]See Taylor, *St. Mark*, 423; Best, *Following*, 107-108; and Fleddermann, "Discipleship Discourse," 61ff.

10 ¹³And they were bringing children to him, that he might touch them; and the disciples rebuked them. ¹⁴But when Jesus saw it he was indignant, and said to them, "Let the children come to me, do not hinder them; for to such belongs the Kingdom of God. ¹⁵Truly, I say to you, whoever does not receive the Kingdom of God like a child shall not enter it." ¹⁶And he took them in his arms and blessed them, laying his hands upon them.

Later Christian tradition will see in this passage a text that supports infant baptism, although this is not the use intended by Mark.³⁴ The main thrust of this story in its present location is not about the need to bring children to Jesus for baptism or anything else. The story has to do with the need for all who would be disciples of Jesus to receive the Kingdom as a child receives.

The child, therefore, is a very important symbol in this section of Mark's Gospel. The child symbolizes both the needy person the disciple of Jesus must serve (9:36-37) and the type of person the disciple must become (10:13-16). But what is it about the way a child receives that Jesus is drawing attention to in these verses? Most commentators point to the fact that in the eyes of the ancient world a child was considered of little importance and had no social status. Since children were powerless and no one in society owed them anything, everything they received was a result of the love and generosity of their parents or other adults. In this Markan pericope, then, Jesus is telling his followers that one must receive the Kingdom of God as a gift from God. This demand for openness and acceptance is reminiscent of Jesus' first words in Mark's Gospel (1:14-15), where his call for faith includes the element of trust.

While it is not obvious that Mark has infant baptism in mind in these verses, it does seem clear that he understands

³⁴G. R. Beasley-Murray, *Baptism in the New Testament* (Grand Rapids: Eerdmans, 1962) 320ff. For a different view see Jeremias, *Infant Baptism*, 49ff., and O. Cullmann, *Baptism in the New Testament* (London: SCM, 1950) 25f., 71-80.

children to be part of the Christian community. Jesus' acceptance and blessing of the children (10:13-16), his comments that children should be received in his name (9:37), and the inclusion of children in the list of new relations one will receive in his new community (10:29-30), all support this conclusion.[35] In addition to including Jew and Gentile and male and female, Mark's picture of the Christian community also includes both children and adults.

The disciples, therefore, have erred in trying to keep the children from Jesus. They have also made a serious mistake in their selection of role models. These followers of Jesus look at the world in which they live and seek greatness, power, and glory, according to the world's standards. Instead of modeling their behavior after the rich and powerful in the Greco-Roman world, Jesus tells them that they should look to the children. It is everyone, even children, who must be the object of one's service. And children provide the model for how one must accept the Kingdom of God, as a freely given gift.

POSSESSIONS

While it is universally recognized that Luke sharply intensifies the demand for renunciation of earthly posessions which he found in his Markan source, what is often overlooked when the spotlight is focused on Luke is that he obviously found this emphasis on renunciation in the tradition he took over from Mark. The pericope which immediately follows Jesus' blessing of the children, the rich man (10:17-31), examined previously, will be used here as a springboard for a more thorough discussion of Mark's attitude toward the problem of wealth. This rich man is the only person in Mark's Gospel who is specifically told that abandoning all personal possessions is a requirement of discipleship.

[35]It has also been suggested that, since this pericope which mentions children follows immediately after a passage dealing with marriage, Mark is making some comment about the importance of children in a marriage. There is little evidence that this is Mark's intent here.

As was mentioned earlier, Mark seems to view the command to "sell what you have" as a single incident and does not turn it into a general requirement for all would-be followers of Jesus.[36] The following verses (10:23-31), however, do expand the warning about wealth to all rich people. Jesus does not say explicitly that that is impossible for the rich to enter the Kingdom of God, but his hyperbolic comparison of a camel (Palestine's largest animal) passing through a needle's eye (smallest of commonly known openings) implies that it is virtually impossible. The addition of these last few verses (10:23-25) has the effect of changing the focus of the entire pericope. Instead of concentrating on one individual, his possessions, and Christian discipleship, the passage now focuses on rich people in general, their possessions, and entry into the Kingdom of God. Mark's ultimate interest, therefore, is wider than Christian discipleship. Since, as we admitted earlier, one can enter the Kingdom of God without becoming a disciple of Jesus, the question here is whether or not anyone can enter the Kingdom of God without abandoning his/her possessions. Can the rich be saved?

The example of the initial companions of Jesus, as was seen earlier, is very powerful. Although they are not explicitly required to do so, these disciples abandon their possessions in order to follow Jesus on his way. We see that disciples leave behind their families, occupations, and possessions when Jesus calls the four Galileans, Simon, Andrew, James, and John, as they are going about their daily activities as fishermen (1:16-20). Levi also leaves his occupation behind as he rises from his desk at the tax office to follow Jesus (2:14). This supports our earlier conclusion that the Twelve are symbolic of all disciples. It is not only future members of the Twelve, but disciples in general, who choose to join Jesus in his itinerant ministry and his life of voluntary poverty.

The story of the Widow's Mite (12:41-44) also teaches by

[36]But see L. Schottroff and W. Stegemann, *Jesus von Nazareth. Hoffnung der Armen* (Stuttgrt: Kohlhammer, 1978) 99, who argue that the command to sell all that one has is directed to all who are called to full-time discipleship, at least during the ministry of Jesus.

example as it suggests that the rich face great difficulties in their attempt to enter the Kingdom of God. Although the rich people in this passage are following the prescriptions of the law as they bring their gifts for the poor to the Temple treasury, they are not singled out by Jesus for praise. In contrast to these rich people who, according to Mark, are depositing rather large sums of money into the treasury (12:41), is the poor widow who drops in λεπτὰ δύο, two of the smallest denomination of copper coins in use in Palestine at the time.[37] After watching the proceedings Jesus says, "Truly, I say to you, this poor widow has put in more than all those who are contributing to the treasury. For they all contributed out of their abundance; but she out of her poverty has put in everything she had, her whole living" (12:43-44). The widow is seen as a truly religious person whose entire being, including her attitude toward wealth, is affected as she strives to hear and do the will of God. The passage is usually understood to recommend unconditional sharing with the poor and total dependence on God. Although the rich people in this pericope do contribute large sums of money, their abundance does not appear to be threatened. What matters is not how much one gives, but the amount that one keeps for oneself. This interpretation does present us with a potential problem however. After the widow puts her coins into the treasury she is destitute. Does Mark want his readers to take the example of the widow literally?

What does the example of Jesus himself teach us in this regard? Jesus breaks with his family, home, and occupation[38] in order to preach that the Kingdom of God has arrived (3:31-35). When he sends the Twelve out on their missionary travels (6:7-13) he instructs them to take nothing for their journey except a staff: no bread, no bag, and no money. They are to avoid appearing like other missionaries in the Greco-Roman world, who make a good living out of their preaching. Their lack of possessions indicates that they believe God will

---

[37]H. Hamburger, "Money, Coins," *IDB* 3, 428.

[38]Mark tells us that Jesus was a carpenter (6:3).

sustain them on their missionary journey. Jesus also commands them to accept the hospitality of those who welcome them and to be content with it. They are not to move from one place to another looking for better conditions; they are to accept whatever is offered to them (6:10). Those who engage in the missionary enterprise without resources are dependent on the grace of God and the good will of the community to which they go.

Jesus' interpretation of the Parable of the Sower (4:13-20) makes abundantly clear the dangers of wealth. He tells his audience that sometimes the word of God, which enters a person like a seed, is unfruitful in the end. The cares of the world, delight in riches, and the desire for other things represent dangers to the would-be disciple. While hearing the word of God is very important, if it does not lead to the production of fruit then such hearing is in vain (cf. 3:35). These verses teach quite clearly that concern for material things can impede one's entry into the Kingdom of God.

These stories about Jesus, the widow, the disciples, and the rich man point unambiguously to the tension which exists between wealth and Christian discipleship. They could be read as implying that the total abandonment of all one's possessions is necessary for anyone who would enter the Kingdom of God; however, the following passages suggest that Mark's teaching on discipleship and possessions is less radical than this, but only slightly so.

We mentioned earlier that Jesus' words in defense of the woman who anoints him at the house of Simon the leper (14:3-9) are frequently misunderstood. Jesus defends the service that this woman has rendered to him, against the charges that the valuable ointment should have been sold and the proceeds given to the poor, when he says, "Let her alone; why do you trouble her? She has done a beautiful thing to me. For you always have the poor with you, and whenever you will, you can do good to them; but you will not always have me" (14:6-7). In light of Deuteronomy 15:11 ("For the poor will never cease out of the land; therefore I command you, You shall open wide your hand to your relatives, to the needy and to the poor, in the land"), these objections to the woman's actions are appropriate. Because of the impending death of Jesus, however, normally inappropriate actions are considered acceptable. The important point here is that this passage does not support the claim that to be a disciple of Jesus one must sell all that one has in order to serve the poor. It is more likely that Mark intended this woman to be seen as an example of service, than an example of giving all that she had. Although this scene presents us with a unique case within the ministry of Jesus, it is quite clear that he does not always require that everything be sold and the proceeds given to the poor.

The Corban saying in Mark 7:10-13 also seems to set limits on giving. In their zeal to follow their religious traditions, the scribes and Pharisees find themselves in opposition to the will of God. Apparently they claim it is permissible to evade one's obligations to one's parents by dedicating money to God that could have been used to care for one's parents. Jesus' comments can be seen to indicate that human needs take precedence over religious obligations (cf. 3:1-5). With this in mind it is reasonable to suggest that Mark does not intend the actions of the widow (12:44), discussed above, to be taken literally.[39] Although these verses (14:3-9; 7:10-13) do not teach that disciples must be destitute, neither do they support any claim that wealth and Christian discipleship are compatible.

The story of the Gerasene demoniac (5:1-20) also shows us that Jesus did not always insist that his supporters leave everything in order to follow him. After he is cured by Jesus, the man who had been possessed with demons wants to accompany Jesus on his way. He begs Jesus to be allowed to join him, but Jesus refuses saying, "Go home to your friends, and tell them how much the Lord has done for you, and how he has had mercy on you" (5:18-19). Because this individual both proclaims ($\kappa\eta\rho\acute{\upsilon}\sigma\sigma\epsilon\iota\nu$) and engages in what appears to be missionary, tasks assigned to the Twelve (3:14-15;

---

[39]See A. G. Wright, "The Widow's Mite: Praise or Lament? A Matter of Context," *CBQ* 44 (1982) 256-265, who argues that Jesus' comment about the widow's action contains words of lament and not praise.

6:7-13), he fulfills many of the requirements of discipleship.[40] Mark thus gives his readers a clear example of someone who has drawn near to the Kingdom without having had to leave either friends or home. The fact that this man's subsequent actions resemble those of Jesus' earlier disciples, as he goes throughout the Decapolis proclaiming how much Jesus has done for him, does not alter the thrust of Jesus' words. While conversion appears to involve the responsibility to evangelize, apparently this can be done in one's hometown among one's friends. The actual physical abandonment of one's friends, family, home, and possessions does not seem to be a prerequisite for discipleship.

While these passages suggest that, according to Mark, one does not have to be destitute and without friends in order to enter into the Kingdom of God, they give no indication that wealth and Christian discipleship are at all compatible. Does this mean that Mark provides a negative answer to our earlier question concerning the possibility of salvation for the rich? Before we accept this as our conclusion let us look once again at the story of the Rich Man (10:17-31).

We saw above that the "great possessions" of this rich man were an insurmountable barrier between him and the Kingdom of God (10:17-22). Jesus indicates in the next few verses (10:23-25) that "riches" present the same problem for their owners when he says, "It is easier for a camel to go through the eye of a needle than for a rich person to enter the Kingdom of God." This saying has been subject to many ingenious interpretations usually designed to obscure its obvious meaning. The most famous of these interpretations are: (1) Jesus originally said $\kappa\acute{\alpha}\mu\iota\lambda o\varsigma$ (rope, cable, or ship's hawser) and not $\kappa\acute{\alpha}\mu\eta\lambda o\varsigma$ (camel). This is widely recognized

---

[40]The fact that the man is sitting (5:15) when the townspeople approach could also suggest that Mark views him as a disciple (cf. 5:18). The implication is that this individual is seated at Jesus' feet, listening to what he has to say. This is the typical position of a disciple.

as an attempt to tone down the meaning of the saying,[41] and makes no contribution toward solving the problem, since neither a camel nor a large rope will go through a needle's eye. (2) There was a gate in the city wall of Jerusalem that was called and/or shaped like the eye of a needle. The conclusion here is that if a long-legged camel stooped to its knees, it could in fact squeeze through such an opening. This interpretation, which does not appear until the ninth century, is considered fanciful by scholars, especially since no such gate is known to have existed.[42]

The conclusion we are left with is that Jesus is using a typical oriental image to emphasize that entry into the Kingdom of God is completely impossible for the rich. This would seem to be the proper interpretation since not only Mark, but Matthew and Luke as well, clearly understand this saying in this way. In all three Synoptic Gospels the question is immediately raised, "Who then can be saved?" The assumption is that the rich cannot be saved. If rich people, who seem to be able to have anything that they want in life, find it virtually impossible to enter the Kingdom, then who can be saved? The response in Mark 10:27 (Mt. 19:26; Lk. 18:27) further underscores this assumption: "With human beings it [the salvation of the rich] is impossible, but not with God; for all things are possible with God."

In what way is salvation of the rich possible with God? Two popular suggestions, both of which take the sharp edge off Jesus' words, are: (1) These verses should be seen as a comfort to the rich, because they tell the rich that God will find a way to save them with their wealth intact. This interpretation is obviously inconsistent with what Mark says elsewhere about wealth and Christian discipleship. Jesus' words on voluntary poverty appear to constitute a strict obligation for the

---

[41]B. M. Metzger, *A Textual Commentary on the Greek New Testament* (New York: United Bible Societies, 1971) 169; Taylor, *St. Mark*, 431; Achtemeier, *Invitation*, 149; and D. Malone,"Riches and Discipleship: Mark 10:23-31," *BTB* 9 (1979) 80.

[42]See e.g., O. Michel, κάμλος" *TDNT* 3, 592-594; Taylor, *St. Mark*, 431; Nineham, *Saint Mark*, 275; Achtemeier, *Invitation*, 149; and Malone, "Riches," 80.

Christian; there is no indication that they are optional, each Christian being free to accept or reject them.[43] (2) Jesus is simply stating a general theological truth, salvation depends on the gracious gift of God and not on human effort. While it is true that salvation comes ultimately from God, this does not mean that a Christian's attitude toward possessions is irrelevant. The result of interpreting these words of Jesus as saying that virtually any attitude toward riches is acceptable for a Christian would be, in effect, to contradict Mark's teaching elsewhere on the proper Christian attitude toward wealth.

All attempts to soften this hard saying of Jesus seem to contradict Mark's clear intent. The subject throughout 10:17-31 is the problem of wealth in relation to the Kingdom of God. The fact that the dsisciples are reported as being "amazed" (10:24) and "exceedingly astonished" (10:26) at Jesus' words, together with their question concerning who can be saved (10:26), suggest that they believe the prosperity of the rich to be a sign of God's blessing. Mark, however, has presented wealth as a stumbling block or an insurmountable barrier on the way to the Kingdom of God. Can the rich be saved?

In the verses under discussion (10:23ff.) Jesus points out that salvation of the rich is possible, but it is possible only through the power of God (10:27). The point of this saying is that God will have to work the miracle of conversion in the hearts of the rich in order for them to be saved. It is so hard for those who have wealth to divest themselves of their material possessions, and the power and security that seem to come with them, that it will take divine intervention to free the rich from their bondage. Riches represent such a barrier; they are so difficult for a person to let go of, that the only way the rich can be saved is by taking advantage of God's grace and ceasing to trust in possessions. If they are to enter the Kingdom of God, rich people must take the steps necessary to cease being egocentric and to begin living for others. They

[43]P. J. Riga, "Poverty as Counsel and as Precept," *TBT* 65 (1973) 1127.

must be freed from their enslavement to material goods and possessions. They must be free to use their riches properly, in the service of all.

The verses which follow (10:28-31) support this interpretation as they direct the reader's attention to a group of individuals, Peter and the disciples, who have overcome the temptation of possessions and left their friends, families, homes, and occupations to follow Jesus in a life of discipleship. Only those who have overcome their selfishness and left their possessions behind are offered the promise of the Kingdom (10:30). This does not mean, however, that one must be destitute in order to be a disciple. Jesus promises that those who forsake all for the Kingdom will receive a hundredfold even in this life. Houses and lands, part of the good things of God's creation, are also included among these benefits of discipleship. Despite his life of voluntary poverty, Jesus is not an ascetic. He states that the Jewish fasting laws should be suspended during his earthly ministry (2:19), he enjoins children to support their parents (7:9-13), and he eats at the tables of Levi (2:15-17) and Simon the leper (14:3-9). The life of the poor, with its hardships and sufferings, is not set forth in Mark's Gospel as an ideal for the Christian disciple, but neither is the desire for possessions nor the accumulation of wealth a reflection of the will of God.

Possessions are not portrayed as evil in themselves, but Mark does think that they have a tremendous potential to become demonic. Wealth can be used for good, but in most cases it creates priorities which prohibit the rich from doing the will of God.

Prayer

The person who investigates the New Testament relationship between Christian discipleship and prayer will arrive inevitably at Luke's two-volume work. The author of Luke-Acts has often been called "the evangelist of prayer" because the theme is such a significant element in the Lukan writings. This emphasis on prayer in Luke-Acts has had the same effect as the scholarly focus on possessions in Luke-Acts; the relationship between discipleship and prayer in Mark frequently has been overlooked. The fact is that Mark's Gospel speaks of prayer in numerous places.

There are at least eight occasions on which Mark draws attention to the prayer life of Jesus (1:35; 6:41, 46; 7:34; 8:6f.; 14:22f., 32-39; 15:34). As early as the first chapter, after he has been healing and exorcising demons and before he announces his preaching tour, we learn that Jesus rises early in the morning and goes out to a lonely place to pray (1:35).[44] Following the Feeding of the 5,000 Jesus makes his disciples get into a boat and set sail for the other side of the Sea of Galilee. He then dismisses the crowd and goes off on his own "into the hills to pray" (6:46). In the middle of his healing of the deaf-mute (7:34) Jesus looks up to heaven before he issues the command, "Be opened." The use of $\dot{\alpha}\nu\alpha\beta\lambda\epsilon\pi\epsilon\iota\nu$ (to look up) here and in 6:41 indicates the act of prayer.[45] Both feeding stories, in Mark's Gospel, as well as the Last Supper pericope, refer to Jesus' prayer life. This is evident (1) in the use of $\epsilon\upsilon\chi\alpha\rho\iota\sigma\tau\epsilon\hat{\iota}\nu$ (to give thanks), in the Feeding of the 4,000 (8:6) and the Last Supper (14:23), and (2) in the use of $\epsilon\upsilon\lambda o\gamma\epsilon\hat{\iota}\nu$ (to invoke a blessing, give thanks/praise) on those same occasions (8:7; 14:22) and in the Feeding of the 5,000 (6:41). Probably the most famous instance where Mark refers to the prayer life of Jesus is in the Gethsemane pericope. Before his arrest, Jesus once again (as in 1:35 and 6:46) separates from his disciples to pray (14:32-39). It is also possible to understand the last words of Jesus in the Gospel of Mark, the words from Psalm 22 that Jesus utters as he hangs on the cross (15:34), as the prayer of a righteous sufferer who still trusts fully in the love and protection of God.[46]

On the basis of Mark's use of language related to prayer we can conclude that: (1) Mark understands communion with

[44]Mark uses the verb $\pi\rho o\sigma\epsilon\upsilon\chi\epsilon\sigma\theta\alpha\iota$ (to pray, make petition) ten times (1:35; 6:46; 11:24, 25; 12:40; 13:18; 14:32, 35, 38, 39) and the substantive $\pi\rho o\sigma\epsilon\upsilon\chi\eta$ (prayer) twice (9:29; 11:17).

[45]Taylor, *St. Mark*, 355.

[46]Nineham, *Saint Mark*, 428-429, and C. W. F. Smith, "Prayer," *IDB* 3, 862f.

God as a feature of the prayers of Jesus. On several occasions, Jesus separates himself from the crowds and from his disciples in order to engage in private communication with God (1:35; 6:46; 14:32-39). In a uniquely Markan contribution to Jesus' Gethsemane prayer, the author portrays Jesus as using the intimate Αββά (father) to refer to God (14:36). (2) The theme of prayer is closely associated with the mission motif. Jesus prays before he embarks on his preaching ministry throughout Galilee (1:35) and before his second thrust into Gentile territory (6:46). Mission and prayer are also associated in the feeding stories (6:41; 8:6f.) and in the miracles of Jesus, which give evidence of God's rule on earth (7:34). (3) In both feeding stories (6:41; 8:6, 7) and at the Last Supper (14:22, 23) Jesus delivers a table blessing. The word "thanksgiving" is usually employed to describe a prayer that functions in this manner. (4) The use of ευ'λογεῖν by those present at Jesus' entry into Jerusalem (11:9-10) and Mark's comment after Jesus healed the paralytic, that "all were amazed and glorified (δοξάζειν) God" (2:12), suggest that, according to Mark, prayer can also be used to praise. But prayer is not all praise and thanksgiving; there must also be a place for (5) petition and intercession. Mark seems to see prayer functioning in this way in 11:24-25 when Jesus says, "Therefore I tell you, whatever you ask in prayer, believe that you will receive it, and you will. And whenever you stand praying, forgive, if you have anything against anyone; so that your Father also who is in heaven may forgive your trespasses." The eschatological prayer that the tribulation may not happen in winter (13:8), Jesus' prayer in Gethsemane (14:32-39), and his urging that Peter, James, and John "watch and pray" that they may not enter into temptation (14:38) also should be considered petitions and pleas for divine intercession. (6) Jesus expects that his followers will pray (11:24-25; 14:38), and in one case we learn that the disciples are unable to effect a miracle because of their unfaithfulness in prayer (9:29). (7) Apparently certain exorcisms can be performed only by prayer (9:29). (8) Mark relates the cleansing of the Temple in terms of Isaiah 56:7, including the fact that God's house is intended as "a house of prayer for all the nations" (11:17).

Although he does not emphasize prayer as much as Luke does, it is evident that Mark also believes prayer has an important role to play in the life of the Christian disciple. Prayer is the way one communicates with God. By means of prayer one offers one's commitment to God and receives strength from God to do his will. Jesus seeks such strength after he withdraws to a quiet place before embarking on the next stage in his ministry (1:35; 6:46) and after he separates from his disciples in Gethsemane (14:32-39). He urges his followers to pray that they may be able to endure their own times of tribulation (13:18; 14:32). Prayer makes possible some exorcisms (9:29), and is an indispensable means for fulfilling a disciple's needs (11:22-25). The Christian is to pray with confidence, fully expecting that what is requested of God will in fact come to pass.

Conclusion

In this chapter we saw that the Christian community is united and pursuing unity. Mark presents Jesus as a unifier who breaks through ethnic and sexual barriers as he demonstrates that the Kingdom of God is open to all who do the will of God. The ancient liturgical celebrations of Eucharist and baptism are important components of Christian discipleship, but they can be understood correctly only if they are seen as being grounded in the suffering and death of Jesus. Followers of Jesus are likely to be distinguished from the world in which they live by their attitude toward marriage, children, and possessions. The hallmarks of Christian marriage appear to be the equality of husband and wife within the relationship and the belief in the permanence of the marriage bond. Children are seen as an important part of the Christian community; in fact, in their trusting ways and the manner in which they receive gifts they provide a model for discipleship. Personal possessions are to be kept to a minimum. Instead of selfishly accumulating wealth, the disciple is to use such goods for the benefit of others, remembering that like Jesus the Christian is to be a servant of all. Above all, the faithful follower of Jesus is to trust in God. Prayer is the means by which the disciple communicates with God, confidently asking for what one needs and gratefully thanking and praising God for his good gifts.

7

Christology and Discipleship

Thus far we have focused on what a disciple is expected to do, how someone who wishes to follow Jesus ought to behave. But this question, "What does it mean to follow Jesus?" cannot be separated from the question of Jesus' identity, "Who is Jesus?"[1] In one of the most important verses in Mark's Gospel, Jesus himself raises the question when he asks his disciples, "Who do you say that I am?" (8:29). This question to the disciples, which is strategically located at the approximate mid-point of Mark's Gospel, obviously forces one to think about one's own understanding of Jesus. It is also reasonable to assume, therefore, that the Christian disciple is expected to have a correct understanding of Jesus' identity. Scholarly research agrees that Mark himself is very concerned with the question of the correct understanding of Jesus.[2]

---

[1]R. H. Fuller and P. Perkins, *Who Is This Christ?* (Philadelphia: Fortress, 1983) 77.

[2]See Achtemeier, *Mark*, 53, who states that the central problem of Mark's narrative is the problem of Christology. In the first edition of *Mark* (1975), Achtemeier concluded that recent research "has pointed unmistakably to the fact that a major reason—if not *the* major reason—for the writing of Mark centers around this christological problem" (41).

There is an intrinsic connection between Christology and discipleship. To discover Jesus' identity is to learn what true discipleship is, and vice versa. An incorrect understanding of Jesus will obviously result in an inadequate or misdirected following of Jesus. On the other hand, it seems clear that only by following Jesus does one come to understand who Jesus is. Discipleship, therefore, is the precondition for "orthodoxy," not vice versa. This is surely the point of 8:34ff. as a corrective to Peter's inadequate perception of Messiahship in 8:29-33.

A casual reader of Mark's Gospel might see Jesus simply as a magician, not unlike other ancient Near Eastern miracle workers, but he is more than this. It is possible that someone might be impressed by the teaching of Jesus and see him as another Socrates or a famous Jewish rabbi. But to understand Jesus simply as another authoritative teacher is to misunderstand him. It is true that Jesus did work miracles and that he was an authoritative teacher, but he is more than this according to Mark. An immense body of literature has grown up around the question of Jesus' identity (Christology), making a comprehensive survey beyond the scope of this book. But because this is clearly an important issue for Mark, it must concern us. Our approach in this chapter will be to concentrate on the titles Mark uses for Jesus. While a few scholars disagree with this approach,[3] the fact is that Mark does use these titles at strategic points throughout the Gospel. One must not concentrate on these titles in the abstract, of course, but rather pay close attention to how they are used within Mark's story and how they affect his understanding of discipleship.[4]

The three principal Christological titles Mark uses for Jesus are found together in 14:61-62. At the trial of Jesus before the Sanhedrin the high priest asks him, "Are you the Christ, the Son of the Blessed [i.e., God]?" Jesus responds by saying, "I am; and you will see the Son of Man sitting at the

---

[3]See e.g., R.C. Tannehill, "The Gospel of Mark as Narrative Christology," *Semeia* 16 (1979) 57-95, and Kee, *Community*, 116.

[4]J.D. Kingsbury, *The Christology of Mark's Gospel* (Philadelphia: Fortress, 1983) ix, 53.

right hand of Power, and coming with the clouds of heaven." The order in which we will examine these Christological titles will conform to the order in which these titles appear in 14:61-62. (1) It seems reasonable to begin our discussion of Markan Christology by looking at how Mark employs the title "Christ," or "Messiah," for Jesus. This is not based solely on the question of the high priest in 14:61, but also on Peter's response to Jesus' question, "Who do you say that I am?" (8:29). Peter answers Jesus by saying, "You are the Christ" (8:30). (2) Since the high priest seems to think that there is a close connection between "Christ" and "Son of the Blessed [i.e., God]," we will next survey Mark's use of the title "Son of God." (3) Although Jesus accepts the titles that the high priest offers him, he seems to provide a further explanation or clarification by immediately speaking about the Son of Man. Our examination of Mark's use of the title "Son of God," therefore, will logically lead into a review of the evangelist's use of the title "Son of Man" for Jesus.

Mark's obvious interest in calling his readers' attention to the suffering and death of Jesus has been pointed out previously. We will be reminded of this Markan interest below when we examine the suffering Son of Man sayings. When the importance of this theme is joined with the recognition that references to Isaiah 42 and 53 lie behind certain Markan texts, an examination of Mark's portrayal of Jesus as the Suffering Servant is in order. Although the title "Servant of the Lord" does not occur in this Gospel, it is clear that this figure also plays an important role in shaping Mark's picture of Jesus.

Markan Christology

THE CHRIST

The term "Christ" comes from the Greek word χριστός which means "anointed," and is a translation of the Hebrew word *mashiah*, which also means anointed. The English terms

"Christ" and "Messiah," therefore, are words which refer to exactly the same thing, an "anointed" person. After a brief look at the Old Testament use of *mashiah* we will survey how Mark employs the word "Christ" in an effort to learn what he understood by the term and how important it was in his presentation of Jesus.

The first thing to recognize is that there was no unanimously agreed upon Jewish doctrine of the Messiah at the time of Jesus.[5] In the Hebrew Scriptures the term "anointed" is used of Israelite kings (Saul, David, and David's successors),[6] a non-Israelite king (Cyrus of Persia),[7] priests (Aaron and his sons),[8] prophets (patriarchs as prophets, Elisha),[9] and the Servant of the Lord.[10] In certain periods of Israelite history there was a vivid hope that a new era would begin under the leadership of an anointed "son of David" (cf. Ps. 89 and Isa. 9-11). After the Babylonian Exile (587-538 B.C.), however, the priestly rulers of Israel, rather than the Davidic king, became the focal point of such future hopes. The Dead Sea Scrolls reveal that at Qumran (ca. 140 B.C.–68 A.D.) there was the expectation of two messiahs, one priestly and one political. Most scholars conclude that the general Jewish expectation at the time of Jesus was for a political king and military leader who would drive out the Romans.[11] Does Mark give us a clear indication of what he understands by "Messiah" and whether or not he thinks this is an important designation for Jesus?

The term "Christ" appears seven times in Mark's Gospel (1:1; 8:29; 9:41; 12:35; 13:21; 14:61; 15:32). The evangelist

[5]O. Cullmann, *The Christology of the New Testament* (trans. S.C. Gutherie and C.A.M. Hall; Philadelphia: Westminster, 1959), 111.

[6]Saul (e.g., 1 Sam. 24:6, 10), David (e.g., 2 Sam. 19:21), and David's successors (e.g., 2 Chr. 6:42, cf. 1 Sam. 2:10).

[7]Isaiah 45:1.

[8]Exodus 28:41; Leviticus 4:3.

[9]Patriarchs as prophets (Ps. 105:15 = 1 Chr. 16:22), and Elijah and Elisha (1 Kgs. 19:15-16).

[10]Isaiah 61:1-2. These verses, which Jesus quotes in Luke 4:18ff., are so similar in spirit to the Servant Songs of Isaiah 40-55 that many include them in the song cycle.

[11]See e.g., Vermes, *Jesus the Jew*, 129-156.

appears to use "Christ" as a personal name and title: (1) in the first verse of the Gospel, when he states that this is "the beginning of the gospel of Jesus Christ, the Son of God (1:1),[12] and (2) in the story of the Strange Exorcist, when Jesus says that whoever gives his disciples a cup of water to drink because they bear the "name of Christ" will be rewarded (9:41). The term "Christ" is again on the lips of Jesus in 12:35 as he questions his audience about their understanding of Psalm 110. The passage assumes that the Psalms were composed by David and that 110:1 ("The Lord says to my lord") refers to the Messiah. It should be noted that, in two of the three passages referred to thus far, χριστός is qualified or explained. "Christ" is both the Son of God (1:1) and the "son of David" (12:35).[13] On two other occasions Mark uses the term "Christ" and then proceeds to define it more precisely: (1) When Jesus is led before Caiaphas (14:61), the high priest asks him if he is "Christ, the Son of the Blessed." (2) When Jesus is hanging on the cross, the bystanders mockingly refer to him as "the Christ, the King of Israel" (15:32). Although the explanation of the term "Christ" changes with the speaker, in each of these cases it appears to be used correctly of Jesus. This conclusion is strengthened when we notice that Mark clearly identifies when the term is being misused. In the apocalyptic speech of Mark 13, for example, we learn that people will rise up in the end-time and falsely claim that they are "the Christ" (13:21f.). Our tentative conclusion, therefore, is that "Christ" ("Messiah") is viewed by Mark as a correct but insufficient title for Jesus.[14]

On two occasions in Mark's Gospel Jesus is directly offered the title "Messiah." His reaction to these offers holds the key

[12]Metzger, *Textual Commentary*, 73, favors the inclusion of "Son of God" here. This is also accepted e.g., by Taylor, *St. Mark*, 152; Kingsbury, *Christology*, 55, n. 43; and N. Perrin, "The High Priest's Question and Jesus' Answer (Mk. 14:61-62)," 83, in *Passion*.

[13]Most scholars believe that Mark understands Jesus to be the son of David. See e.g., J.R. Donahue, "Temple, Trial, and Royal Christology (Mark 14:53-65)," 72ff., in *Passion*, and Kingsbury, *Christology*, 47-155. In *Kingdom*, 95, however, Kelber argues that Mark rejects the idea that Jesus is the son of David.

[14]Kingsbury, *Christology*, 149.

to what Mark thinks about this title as a proper designation for Jesus. The first scene is that dramatic moment which we have referred to previously, when Peter answers Jesus' question, "Who do you say that I am?," by stating "You are the Christ" (8:29).

> [27]And Jesus went on with his disciples, to the villages of Caesarea Philippi; and on the way he asked his disciples, "Who do people say that I am?" [28]And they told him, "John the Baptist; and others say, Elijah; and others one of the prophets." [29]And he asked them, "But who do you say that I am?" Peter answered him, "You are the Christ." [30]And he charged them to tell no one about him.
>
> [31]And he began to teach them that the Son of Man must suffer many things, and be rejected by the elders and the chief priests and the scribes, and be killed, and after three days rise again. [32]And he said this plainly. And Peter took him, and began to rebuke him. [33]But turning and seeing his disciples, he rebuked Peter, and said, "Get behind me, Satan! For you are not on the side of God, but of human beings."

Although most of Jesus' contemporaries consider him a "prophet"(8:28), a title Jesus seems to accept as legitimate (cf. 6:4), Peter confesses that Jesus is "the Christ." Instead of praising Peter for this insight, however, Jesus commands silence. He then proceeds to talk about the Son of Man, not the Messiah, and about suffering and death. Peter refuses to accept this and begins to rebuke Jesus (8:32). Jesus then rebukes Peter saying, "Get behind me, Satan! For you are not on the side of God, but of human beings" (8:33). While some scholars claim that Jesus has rejected the term Messiah here,[15] most do not. Peter's confession is seen as basically correct, yet insufficient since it does not include the idea of suffering. When he has Peter refer to Jesus as "the Christ," Mark

---

[15]See e.g., Weeden, *Traditions*, 64-69, and Kelber, *Kingdom*, 82-83. cf. Nineham, *Saint Mark*, 224-225.

probably expects his readers to understand it in terms of the general Jewish expectation at the time. As mentioned above, this would have meant a political king and military leader who would have come to destroy the Romans and violently establish his glorious Kingdom. Although Jesus does not actually reject the term, he does have some reservations about this title and seems to prefer the title "Son of Man."

The second occasion in Mark where Jesus is offered the title "Messiah" is in his trial before the Sanhedrin (14:61). Jesus answers the question of the high priest, "Are you the Christ, the Son of the Blessed?" (14:61) by saying, "I am; and you will see the Son of Man sitting at the right hand of Power, and coming with the clouds of heaven" (14:62). Mark has the high priest attribute to Jesus two of the major Christological titles of the Gospel, "Christ" and "Son of the Blessed [God]," which Jesus clearly accepts. It must be noted, however, that just as in the Caesarea Philippi scene, Jesus immediately drops any reference to "Christ" and proceeds to talk about the Son of Man.[16]

Our conclusion, then, is that Mark views the term "Christ" as a correct yet insufficient designation for Jesus. The evangelist introduces Jesus to his readers as the Messiah (1:1) and appears to present Jesus as using this term to refer to himself (9:41). On several occasions, however, the term stands in need of elaboration. Mark tells his readers that Jesus is the "Christ" only insofar as this is understood to mean that he is the Son of God (1:1; 14:61), the son of David (12:35), and the king of Israel (15:32). Jesus never enthusiastically accepts this designation and twice (8:31; 14:62) expands upon it by speaking about the Son of Man. In Mark's Gospel, therefore, it appears that Jesus accepts this title as basically correct, yet ultimately in need of further explanation.

The question of Jesus' identity is closely connected with the theme of discipleship. This issue is raised: (1) during the first

---

[16]See Donahue, "Royal Christology," 71, and *Are You The Christ?* (SBLDS 10; Missoula: University of Montana, 1973) 88-95, 177-180; and N. Perrin, "High Priest's Question," 80-95, and *A Modern Pilgrimage in New Testament Christology* (Philadelphia: Fortress, 1974) 84-93, 104-121.

crossing of the Sea of Galilee when the disciples respond to Jesus' stilling of the storm by asking, "Who then is this, that even wind and sea obey him?" (4:41), as well as (2) in the identifications proposed by the Nazareth townspeople,

> **6** ²Where did this man [Jesus] get all this? What is the wisdom given to him? What mighty works are wrought by his hands! ³Is not this the carpenter, the son of Mary and brother of James and Joses and Judas and Simon, and are not his sisters here with us?" And they took offense at him.

and, (3) by Herod, in language similar to that of 8:28,

> **6** ¹⁴Some said, "John the baptizer has been raised from the dead; that is why these powers are at work in him." ¹⁵But others said, "It is Elijah." And others said, "It is a prophet, like one of the prophets of old." ¹⁶But when Herod heard of it he said, "John, whom I beheaded has been raised."

The inadequacy of Peter's answer in 8:29(32) is not just an intellectual failure, therefore, but above all a failure to recognize what following Jesus is all about.

The implications of Jesus' modification of the title "Messiah" for discipleship are found in 8:34-38. In these verses, discussed earlier, we learn that discipleship involves something radically different from the violent overthrow of the Roman government. Christian discipleship entails denying oneself and taking up one's cross and following Jesus. One must adopt a lifestyle in which faithfulness to Jesus and the gospel are more important than one's own life. Material wealth and possessions cannot be allowed to interfere with this total commitment to Jesus, and one must not be ashamed of either Jesus or his words. This is a rather serious matter since one's eternal destiny depends on having the correct understanding of "Messiah" and on putting into practice the kind of discipleship which results from this understanding.

SON OF GOD

As we have just seen, on two occasions when Mark elaborates upon the term "Christ" he refers to Jesus as the "Son of God" (1:1; 14:61). Although some argue that "Son of Man" (which will be examined below) is the most important title for Jesus in Mark,[17] most acknowledge that "Son of God" is the supreme Christological title in the Gospel.[18] Before we examine how Mark uses this title, we must comment briefly on: (1) several modern misunderstandings of this title, and (2) the background of this pre-Markan term.

It has been pointed out that modern readers frequently misunderstand what Mark means by the title "Son of God."[19] (1) As the result of reading Homer's *Iliad*, or other works of Greek mythology, some arrive at the mistaken conclusion that Jesus became the Son of God as the result of a physical begetting. Although this view is not usually held by Christians, it is important for us to realize that some people we encounter will see little difference between the Christian claim that Jesus is both the "Son of God" and the "Son of Mary" (6:3) and Homer's story in which Achilles is both the son of the sea goddess Thetis and the mortal man Peleus. The Semitic background of the title "Son of God" makes this interpretation impossible. "For the Lord to have intercourse with a female consort or a human being was absolutely repugnant to the Hebrew faith."[20] (2) Some post-Nicene Christians, on the other hand, are tempted to interpret "Son of God" by using terms like "being" and "substance," which are derived from

[17]See Weeden, *Traditions*, 65, n. 20, who claims that "The Son-of-man title is the only christological title in Mark that is not censored or cloaked in secrecy" and Achtemeier, *Mark*, who admits the importance of the title "Son of God" (34), yet concludes that for Mark the title "Son of Man" is the one most adequate to express the meaning of Jesus of Nazareth (58). See also P.J. Achtemeier, " 'He Taught Them Many Things': Reflections on Marcan Christology," *CBQ* 42 (1980) 465-481.

[18]See e.g., Perrin, *Pilgrimage*, 78, 84-85; L.S. Hay, "The Son-of-God Christology in Mark," *JBR* 32 (1964) 106-114; Kelber, *Kingdom*, 80-81; and Kingsbury, *Christology*, 144.

[19]See Reumann, *Jesus*, 286-290.

[20]*Ibid.*, 289.

Greek metaphysics. References to "Son of God" in the Old Testament, however, denote a moral and functional relationship, not a metaphysical one. Against the background of the Hebrew Scriptures, the title "Son of God" means being chosen or elected to a task, thus participating in the work of God; it implies obedience, the obedience of a son to a father."[21] This does not mean that functional Christology and ontological Christology are mutually exclusive. It does mean, however, that the priority of functional Christology must always be maintained and that ontological Christology "must never lose sight of the fact that it is subsequent reflection on the problems posed by the first type."[22] (3) Some modern readers distort this important Christological term by claiming that we are all sons and daughters of God. A survey of how "Son of God" is used in the Old Testament, the Dead Sea Scrolls, and Mark's Gospel clearly indicates that something more is intended than the observation that we are all children of God.

Since the turn of the century several scholars have suggested that the term "Son of God" is to be interpreted against the background of the Hellenistic concept of "divine man" ($\theta\varepsilon\hat{\imath}o\varsigma$ '$\alpha\nu\acute{\eta}\rho$).[23] This figure was seen as a superman, a human figure endowed with divine powers. He was not a deity himself, but because he was a combination of the divine and human he was seen as superhuman. As $\theta\varepsilon\hat{\imath}o\varsigma$ '$\alpha\nu\acute{\eta}\rho$, this figure possessed extraordinary gifts and abilities, especially in the areas of divine wisdom and power. He possessed supernatural knowledge and intervened in human affairs to work miracles on behalf of human beings.[24]

The scholarly debate on this issue continues, but most have become more cautious than they once were. Now it is

[21]*Ibid.*, 290; See also Cullmann, *Christology*, 270.

[22]Fuller and Perkins, *Who Is This Christ?*, 11.

[23]For a recent discussion of the scholarly debate, see Kingsbury, *Christology*, 25ff.

[24]See Weeden, *Traditions*, 55; P.J. Achtemeier, "Gospel Miracle Tradition and the Divine Man," *Int* 26 (1972) 186-187; and Kingsbury, *Christology*, 27.

assumed that: (1) when Mark wrote, θεῖος 'ανήρ was not a fixed concept with a definite, well-known meaning, and (2) Mark's use of the title of Son of God is not clearly dependent on the use of θεῖος 'ανήρ in Hellenistic Judaism.[25] Since the title "Son of God" appears in the Old Testament with various meanings, scholarly attention has shifted to the evidence that supports a Semitic background for the title "Son of God."

It is well known that "Son of God" is applied in the Old Testament to: (1) the nation of Israel (Ex. 4:22; Hos. 11:1), (2) the king, as the leader and symbol of the nation (2 Sam. 7:14), and (3) other figures who receive some special commission from God (e.g. ministering angels in Dan. 3:25, 28). The problem with this line of inquiry has always been in its inability to provide convincing evidence that the term "Son of God" was used as a title for the Messiah in pre-Christian Judaism. With the discovery and translation of texts from Qumran, however, the situation has changed slightly. Some now argue that because the title "Son of God" is attested in a Qumran text (4QFlor 10-13) it can be understood in a Messianic sense.[26] While one should be cautious about claiming too much for this text,[27] it is clear that scholarly consensus is moving away from the θεῖος 'ανήρ position to the belief that Mark's use of the "Son of God" to refer to the "Messiah" depends primarily on the Old Testament background of the title and the traditions that develop from it. As stated earlier, against this background the term "Son of God" denotes primarily a moral and functional relationship to God. To be the "Son of God" means to be obedient to the will of God.

---

[25]So Holladay, *Theos* Anēr, 1-15, who is followed by both Kingsbury, *Christology*, 35, and Fuller and Perkins, *Who Is This Christ?*, 48.

[26]R. H. Fuller, *The Foundations of New Testament Christology* (New York: Scribner's, 1965) 32; M. Black, "The Christological Use of the Old Testament in the New Testament," *NTS* 18 (1971/72) 2-4; and C. F. D. Moule, *The Origins of Christology* (Cambridge: Cambridge University, 1977) 28.

[27]See J. A. Fitzmyer, *A Wandering Aramean* (SBLMS 25; Missoula: Scholars, 1979) 105-106, and *The Gospel According To Luke I-IX* (Garden City: Doubleday, 1981) 338-339.

The implications of Jesus' designation as the Son of God for discipleship are clear when one examines the new family texts of 3:35 and 10:29-30. Jesus is God's Son (3:11), and those who do God's will are brother, sister, and mother of Jesus (3:35). The omission of a new father in 10:30 implies that one's relationship to Jesus the Son results in a filial relationship to his Father. Just as the Son of God is obedient to the will of God, so must those he calls brother, sister, and mother be obedient to God's will.

The title "Son of God" does not occur very frequently in Mark's Gospel, but each use is extremely important. Mark tells his readers in the first verse of the Gospel that Jesus is the Son of God (1:1). There is no reason to doubt what the evangelist tells us as he begins his Gospel so, just as we assumed above that Jesus was indeed the Christ, we accept as reliable information Mark's statement that Jesus is the Son of God. The truth of the evangelist's comment is reinforced when God enters the story. Although God only appears twice in the Gospel as an actor, both times it is to declare that Jesus is his beloved Son (1:11 and 9:7). The designation of Jesus as the Son of God is further supported by the comments of the other supernatural beings in the story, the demons. Mark tells his readers that Jesus "would not permit the demons to speak, because they knew him" (1:34). Because of this assurance from the narrator it is reasonable to conclude that the demons are correct when they refer to Jesus as the "Holy One of God" (1:24), the "Son of God" (3:11), and the "Son of the Most High God" (5:7). Mark even seems to have Jesus identify himself as the Son of God: (1) in the apocalyptic speech, when he says, "But of that day or that hour no one knows, not even the angels in heaven, nor the Son, but only the Father" (13:32), and (2) in the Parable of the Wicked Tenants, when he speaks about the "beloved son" who will be killed (12:1-11). The last two instances in the Gospel where Jesus is referred to as the Son of God are before the Sanhedrin, when the high priest asks Jesus if he is the Son of the Blessed (14:61), and at the crucifixion, when the centurion says "Truly this man was the Son of God!" (15:39). This confession by the centurion is widely seen as the Christological high point of the Gospel.[28]

It is the dead body of the crucified Jesus that is recognized as the Son of God (by one of his crucifiers, no less). This suggests that the place to perceive Jesus' Sonship is not first of all in glory, elevation, etc., but in his suffering and death. "Son of God," like "Christ," is reinterpreted to fit into Mark's primary focus on suffering. In a sense this is already foreshadowed at the baptism: (1) when the voice proclaims Jesus' Sonship at the very point of abasement, as he identifies with the poor, broken, sinful people coming to be baptized, and (2) where the Messianism of Psalm 2:7 is modified by Isaiah 42.

Appearing as they do, at the beginning, the middle, and the end of Gospel, Mark's references to Jesus as the Son of God have been called the frame around which the basic Christological structure of the Gospel is arranged.[29] At the baptism of Jesus by John, the heavenly voice uses words from Psalm 2:7 and Isaiah 42:1 to identify Jesus as God's beloved Son (1:11). He is again identified as God's beloved Son in the Transfiguration account (9:7) which occurs at the midpoint of the Gospel. The final time Jesus is referred to as the Son of God, according to Mark, is at the moment of his death when the centurion at the foot of the cross identifies Jesus as the Son of God (15:39).

As in the baptism scene and in the centurion's words, there are obvious implications for discipleship in the account of the Transfiguration. The words of God, "This is my beloved Son," are addressed to the three disciples and are followed by the command "listen to him" (9:7). The disciple must listen to the words of Jesus, the Son of God. This injunction is followed by a discussion between Jesus and his disciples which clearly places this event in the context of the Passion (9:9-13). Perhaps this is what they are called on to "listen to"

[28]Perrin, *Pilgrimage*, 78, 85, 115; Reumann, *Jesus*, 287; Nineham, *Saint Mark*, 431; Taylor, *St. Mark*, 597-598; and Kingsbury, *Christology*, 47-155 *passim*.

[29]Perrin, *Pilgrimage*, 85.

in particular. Certainly there are implications for discipleship here. The suffering Messiahship of Jesus, with its complement, suffering discipleship, is again emphasized.

"Son of God" is the only title in Mark which is applied to Jesus by both human and transcendent beings. It is used by God (1:11; 9:7), the demons (3:11; 5:7; cf. 1:24), Jesus (12:6; 13:32; cf. 14:62), the high priest (14:61), and the centurion (15:39). This title, which denotes the filial relationship between Jesus and God, originates in the royal Messianism of Israel[30] and serves to bind together the titles "Christ," "son of David," and "king of the Jews (Israel),"[31] in Mark's Gospel.

SON OF MAN

Although there is no scholarly concensus concerning the importance of the title "Son of Man" in pre-Christian Jewish traditions, there is widespread agreement that "Son of Man" is an important Christological title in Mark's Gospel. In the Old Testament "son of man" is used: (1) generically to mean "human beings" or "humankind" (Ps. 8:4), (2) numerous times in Ezekiel to refer to the prophet who, though a frail human being, has been taken into God's service, and (3) in Daniel 7:13 to denote an apocalyptic, more than human, figure[32] who will come "with the clouds of heaven" (cf. Mk. 14:62) and be given, power, glory and the Kingdom. In the

[30]Donahue, "Royal Christology," 71-78; Kingsbury, *Christology*, 47-155; and F. J. Matera, *The Kingship of Jesus: Composition and Theology in Mark 15* (SBLDS 66; Chico: Scholars, 1982) 62.

[31]All six references in this Gospel to Jesus as the "king of the Jews (Israel)" occur in Mark 15 (15:2, 9, 12, 18, 26, 32). Although Mark has applied texts from Israel's royal Messianic tradition (e.g., Ps. 2:7) to Jesus throughout the Gospel, he has this title applied explicitly to Jesus only in the climactic section of his story, when Jesus true identity is revealed. It is reasonable to suggest that Mark was influenced by the Ancient Near Eastern and Old Testament view of kingship, whereby the king provides especially for the disenfranchised (cf. Ps. 72), in his presentation of the kingship of Jesus.

[32]In the beast allegory of Daniel 7, the "son of man" figure represents Israel as a whole, just as the various animals represent the nations.

intertestamental[33] Jewish book known as 1 Enoch the "Son of Man" appears as an eschatological judge and deliverer who will overthrow the wicked and vindicate the righteous (1 Enoch 46-53).

Mark uses the title "Son of Man" fourteen times in his Gospel, usually in connection with the humiliation, suffering, and death of Jesus. In all three passion-resurrection predictions Jesus tells us that it is necessary for the Son of Man to suffer, die, and rise (8:31; 9:31; 10:33-34). He interprets the passion of the Son of Man as a ransom when he says, "the Son of Man also came not to be served but to serve, and to give his life as a ransom for many" (10:45). Other references to the suffering Son of Man are: (1) Jesus' question after the Transfiguration, "How is it written of the Son of Man, that he should suffer many things and be treated with contempt?" (9:12), (2) Jesus' words at the Last Supper, "For the Son of Man goes as it is written of him, but woe to that man by whom the Son of Man is betrayed! (14:21), and (3) Jesus' comment in Gethsemane that "the hour has come; the Son of Man is betrayed into the hands of sinners" (14:41). Another future-oriented Son of Man saying occurs in 9:9 when Jesus tells the disciples that they should not tell anyone about the Transfiguration until the Son of Man has risen from the dead.

The remaining Son of Man sayings are usually referred to as: (1) apocalyptic sayings and (2) present activity sayings. The former are those which deal with the parousia, the future coming of the Son of Man on the clouds of heaven in great glory. We have already seen apocalyptic language when, in response to the high priest's question, Jesus says, "You will see the Son of Man sitting at the right hand of Power, and coming with the clouds of heaven" (14:62). A similar saying occurs when Jesus notes, "and then they will see the Son of Man coming in clouds with great power and glory" (13:26). Likewise, Jesus speaks after Peter's confession at Caesarea Philippi of a future judgment when the Son of Man will come

[33]The intertestamental period is the time between the events covered in the Old Testament and those reported in the New Testament (i.e., roughly the two centuries before Christ).

"in the glory of his Father with the holy angels" (8:38). The present activity sayings refer to the authority of the Son of Man during his earthly activity. In this category one would include: (1) Jesus' comment that "the Son of Man has authority on earth to forgive sins" (2:10), and (2) his observation that "the Son of Man is lord even of the sabbath" (2:28).

The frequency with which this title is used suggests that it is an important Christological title for Mark. This is supported by: (1) the close association of the title "Son of Man" with the suffering and death of Jesus, already seen as a theme of considerable interest to Mark, and (2) the fact that only Jesus uses this term in Mark's Gospel; neither his disciples nor his enemies refer to Jesus as the Son of Man. This has led a number of scholars to argue that Mark considers the title Son of Man to be the supreme title for Jesus. It is seen as Mark's way of correcting the other Christological titles which he considers defective, erroneous, or ambiguous.[34]

While the Son of Man sayings obviously play an important role in what Mark wants to say about the necessity of the suffering and death of Jesus, we believe that it would be a mistake to see "Son of Man" as the supreme Christological title for Jesus in Mark's Gospel.[35] God enters into Mark's story to announce that Jesus is his "beloved Son" on two occasions, at Jesus' baptism (1:11) and at the Transfiguration (9:7). Since there is no indication that Mark views God as incorrect, it would seem that Jesus is not correcting the high priest's designation of him as the "Son of the Blessed" (14:61) when he immediately refers to the coming of the Son of Man (14:62). It would be better to see Jesus using the Son of Man sayings to elaborate on or expand upon the titles "Christ" and "Son of God." In other words, the title "Christ" is essentially correct, but must be understood to refer to Jesus as the king of Israel and the Son of God. In using the title "Son of Man,"

[34]See Weeden, *Mark*, 64-69; Perrin, *Pilgrimage*, 110-121, and "Mark 14:61-62"; Achtemeier, *Mark*, 58ff., and "'He Taught Them,'" 472, 481; and N.R. Petersen, *Literary Criticism* 63, 67-68, 72, 75.

[35]See Kingsbury, *Christology*, 157-159.

Mark has drawn his readers' attention to the fact that the "Christ," the Davidic king, the "Son of God," must suffer and die. Insofar as any of these titles are understood to exclude humiliation, suffering, and death, they are misunderstood. The title "Son of Man," therefore, complements the other titles; it does not contradict them.

As pointed out above, not every Son of Man saying is concerned with suffering. Mark's identification of Jesus as the Son of Man who will come with power and glory on the clouds of heaven is also important. In the apocalyptic saying of 8:38, however, Jesus speaks about the Son of Man coming "in the glory of his Father with the holy angels." The importance of this saying is not primarily Jesus' self-designation as the Son of Man, but his reference to himself as the Son of God.[36] In this same section of the Gospel we find Peter's Confession (8:29), Jesus' comments about the Passion of the Son of Man (8:31), and the words from heaven at the Transfiguration (9:7). All three scenes are considered by most scholars to be extremely important because they occur approximately at the mid-point of the Gospel. What is often overlooked is the possibility that Mark is expanding upon each title with the one which succeeds it. The most general, yet still correct, title for Jesus would be the one used by Peter, the "Christ" (8:29). Jesus himself becomes more specific as he points out that he is the Son of Man who must suffer, die, and rise (8:31). This progression culminates in the use of the most important of the three major Christological titles for Jesus in Mark's Gospel when, at the Transfiguration, God intervenes to declare that Jesus is his "beloved Son" (9:7).[37] In light of the foregoing, it appears that Son of God is indeed the supreme Christological title for Jesus in Mark's Gospel.

[36]Ibid., 171-173.

[37]The close connection between the titles "Son of God" and "Son of Man" is apparent when the latter recurs in 9:9, 12.

SERVANT OF THE LORD

It is difficult to talk about the suffering Son of Man without thinking about one of the most famous figures in the entire Old Testament, the Suffering Servant of Isaiah 40-55. Whether one concludes that the Son of Man was expected to suffer according to pre-Christian Judaism,[38] that Jesus himself combined the title "Son of Man" with the idea of the Suffering Servant,[39] or that the suffering Son of Man sayings originated in the early church,[40] is not of major concern for our study. What is important for us, and quite obvious, is that by the time Mark writes his Gospel, the Son of Man is a figure who is expected to suffer and die. Behind this picture of the suffering Son of Man are the Psalms of the suffering Just One and the Suffering Servant from Second Isaiah.[41]

The influence of Isaiah 52:13-53:12 on Mark's passion narrative has been recognized for some time.[42] These verses become extremely important: (1) in early Church apologetics, as the Church begins to explain its suffering Messiah, his shameful death (cf. Deut. 21:22-23), and his rejection by his

[38]C.K. Barrett, "The Background of Mark 10:45," in *New Testament Essays: Studies in Memory of T. W. Manson* (ed. A.J.B. Higgins; Manchester: Manchester University, 1959) 1-18, and Reumann, *Jesus,* 277-279.

[39]This is a common British view. See e.g., V. Taylor, *The Names of Jesus* (New York: St. Martin's, 1953) 32-35.

[40]See G. Bornkamm, *Jesus of Nazareth* (trans. I. and F. McLuskey; New York: Harper, 1960) 228; H.E. Tödt, *The Son of Man in the Synoptic Tradition* (Philadelphia: Westminster, 1965); A.J.B. Higgins, *Jesus and the Son of Man* (Philadelphia: Fortress, 1964), and *The Son of Man in the Teaching of Jesus* (SNTSMS 39; Cambridge: Cambridge University, 1980); and R.H. Fuller, *New Testament Christology,* 119-125.

[41]Even if Barrett, "Background," 14, and Reumann, *Jesus,* 277-279, are correct and the Danielic son of man includes the idea of suffering, Mark's portrait of the suffering Son of Man clearly depends on the Servant texts of Second Isaiah. See Higgins, *Jesus,* 47ff.

[42]See J.R. Donahue, "Introduction: From Passion Traditions to Passion Narrative," in, *Passion,* 3-6, who refers to C. H. Dodd, *According to the Scriptures* (New York: Scribner's, 1953) 72, 92-93, 127; W. Zimmerli and J. Jeremias, πᾶις θεοῦ," *TDNT* 5, 654-717, and *The Servant of God* (SBT 20; London: SCM, 1965); and B. Lindars, *New Testament Apologetic* (Philadelphia: Westminster, 1961).

own people,[43] and (2) in early Church soteriology, as the connection is made between the suffering of the Son of Man and the suffering required of disciples who wish to enter the Kingdom of God.[44]

Because what Jesus does arises out of, and can only be understood in terms of, who he is, there is a close connection between Christology and soteriology. As the Servant of the Lord, who is also the suffering-dying-rising Son of Man, Jesus' suffering serves a redemptive purpose. This is seen most clearly in 10:45 and 14:24. When Mark casts Jesus in the role of the Suffering Servant who will "give his life as a ransom for many" (see below), he is using sacrificial terminology. The Servant was expected to atone for the sins of the world by bearing them. Sacrificial language is also used at the Last Supper when Jesus says, "This is my blood of the covenant, which is poured out for many" (14:24). Mark presents Jesus as ratifying in his blood a covenant bond between God and human beings, "a relationship of fellowship and obedience, which is based upon forgiveness, redemption, and reconciliation."[45] The more strictly soteriological implication is that Jesus' suffering and death affect the salvation of the world through the establishment of a new covenant between God and humankind. The connection between the suffering of the Servant of the Lord, who is the Messiah, Son of Man, and Son of God, and the suffering required of disciples is made throughout Mark's Gospel.

As mentioned above, there is little question in scholarly circles that "a ransom for many" (10:45) alludes to Isaiah 53:10-12.[46] The point here is not merely Jesus' identity, but instruction for the disciples in service. Mark has Jesus present suffering servanthood as a model for the disciples to follow, just as he tells them to take up their crosses after the first

---

[43]Lindars, *Apologetic*, 75-76.

[44]Tödt, *Son of Man*, 146-147, and Perrin, *Pilgrimage*, 101-103.

[45]Taylor, *St. Mark*, 124.

[46]Zimmerli and Jeremias, *Servant*, 90 n. 401; Tödt, *Son of Man*, 203; F. Hahn, *The Titles of Jesus in Christology* (New York: World, 1969) 57; Taylor, *Mark*, 444-446; and Perrin, *Pilgrimage*, 94-103.

passion-resurrection prediction (8:34) and to be servants of all after the second passion-resurrection prediction (9:35).

Other, less certain suggestions about connections between Mark's portrait of Jesus and the Servant of the Lord are that: (1) Mark's use of παραδιδόναι (to hand over, deliver up, betray) in two of the passion-resurrection predictions (9:31 and 10:33) and at the Last Supper (14:21; cf. 14:41) refers to Isaiah's words about the Servant: "His soul was delivered up (παρεδόθη) to death" (53:12[LXX]),[47] and (2) Mark's saying about the rejection ('εξουδενηθή) of the Son of Man (9:12) has been influenced by Isaiah 53:3 (LXX), "He was despised and rejected by men" ('εξουδενώμενος in some versions).[48]

In addition to these allusions to Isaiah 53, Mark's passion narrative abounds with references to the Psalms, especially Psalm 22 and other psalms of lamentation.[49] These serve to explain numerous aspects of the Passion and to identify Jesus with the suffering Just One who remains silent (Ps. 38:14-16; 39:9) when false witnesses arise (Ps. 27:12; 35:11; 109:2), his friends betray him (Ps. 55:14-21), and his enemies mock him (Ps. 22:7; 31:11; 35:19-25; 69:20; 109:25) and conspire to kill him (Ps. 31:4; 35:4; 38:12; 71:10).

Evidence that Mark wants his readers to understand Jesus as the suffering Just One and the Suffering Servant is not found only in the passion narrative and in Jesus' sayings. Jesus is acknowledged as the Son of God at his baptism with words from the Servant Song in Isaiah 42:1ff. Since it is generally assumed that the words spoken by God at Jesus'

---

[47]So Zimmerli and Jeremias, *Servant*, 90, 96, and Lindars, *Apologetic*, 80-81. See also Taylor, *St. Mark*, 578. For an opposing view see Tödt, *Son of Man*, 159-161, and Perrin, *Pilgrimage*, 94-103.

[48]So Zimmerli and Jeremias, *Servant*, 90, n. 406, and Lindars, Apologetic, 81, who admit that the Septuagint has 'ητιμάσθη, not 'εξουδενώμενος, but suggest that the variant probably represents an older Palestinian tradition. See Perrin, *Pilgrimage*, 100-101, for an alternative explanation.

[49]Lindars, *Apologetic*, 88-110, and L. Ruppert, *Jesus als der leidende Gerechte* (SBS 59; Stuttgart: Katholisches Bibelwerk, 1972) 16ff., as cited in Donahue, "Introduction," 5.

baptism are a conflation of Psalm 2:7 and Isaiah 42:1,[50] we will take a closer look at these two texts.

The title "Son of God" (Ps. 2:7) is used at the baptism of Jesus in a royal, titulary sense. It characterizes Jesus' installation into the office of king. The remainder of Psalm 2, however, describes the activities of this king in rather violent terms: He will break the nations "with a rod of iron, and dash them in pieces like a potter's vessel" (Ps. 2:9). The contrast between the king of Psalm 2 and the Servant of Isaiah 42 is dramatic. The Servant "will not cry or lift up his voice, or make it heard in the street; a bruised reed he will not break, and a dimly burning wick he will not quench; he will faithfully bring forth justice" (Isa. 42:2-3). The question, then, is which text, Psalm 2 or Isaiah 42, influences Mark's portrait of Jesus? The answer is obvious, Mark presents Jesus not as the warrior-king, but as the Suffering Servant. Jesus is both the Son of God and the Messiah, who is appointed to fulfill the role of the Servant.[51]

Jesus does not seek to bring about the Kingdom of God with great wars of Messianic conquest; in fact, he appears rather weak and insignificant in the eyes of the world. Jesus speaks about his own suffering and death and states that to be his disciple one must be willing to deny oneself, take up one's cross and follow him (8:34). Instead of acting like kings and other rulers, lording power and authority over people, Jesus tells his followers that they must be servants of all (10:43-44; 9:35), just as he has come "to serve, and to give his life as a ransom for many" (10:45).

The great emphasis Mark places on the suffering and death of Jesus in the central section of his Gospel should no longer surprise us. After identifying Jesus as the Son of God in the

---

[50]Taylor, *St. Mark,* 162; Nineham, *Saint Mark,* 62; Lindars, *Apologetic,* 139ff.; A. Feuillet, "The Baptism of Jesus," *TD* 14 (1966) 207; and I.H. Marshall, "Son of God or Servant of Yahweh? — A Reconsideration of Mark 1:11," *NTS* 15 (1968) 335. It is also possible that 1:11 alludes to Genesis 22:2, Isaiah 44:2 and 62:4.

[51]Marshall, "Reconsideration," 336. See also Feuillet, "Baptism," 212, who notes that "the Spirit urges Jesus to begin his mission as the Messiah, more precisely as the suffering servant."

opening verse of the Gospel (1:1), Mark proceeds to define how this title is to be understood in the baptism scene (1:9-11). As he elaborates on this most important Christological title for Jesus, Mark defines "Son of God" in terms of the Suffering Servant. What appears clearly in the mid-section of the Gospel is foreshadowed in the baptism text. The way of Jesus is the way of the Suffering Servant.

Conclusion

We have argued throughout this chapter that who Jesus is cannot be made simply an abstract, speculative matter, but is profoundly concrete and practical. To discover Jesus' identity is to learn what true discipleship is, and vice versa. Our quest, therefore, has been to discover (1) how Mark answers the crucial question of Jesus, "Who do you say that I am?" (8:29) and (2) what implications this understanding of Jesus has for Christian discipleship.

While Mark uses many different titles to refer to Jesus, it is clear that some titles (e.g., Messiah, Son of God, Son of Man) are more important than others (e.g., prophet, son of David, king of Israel). Mark appears to view the title "Messiah" as a correct designation for Jesus, but sees it as inadequate by itself and open to misunderstanding. First-century Judaism expected the Messiah to be a political king or military leader who would violently overthrow the Roman government. Mark agrees that Jesus is the Anointed One whose coming was prophecized in the Old Testament, the Messiah who is the son of David and the king of Israel, but he defines "Messiah" as "the Son of Man who must suffer many things, and be rejected by the elders and the chief priests and the scribes, and be killed, and after three days rise again" (8:31). The implications of this modification of the definition are found in 8:34-38. Discipleship, following the Messiah, means denying oneself and taking up one's cross. It means adopting a lifestyle in which faithfulness to Jesus and the gospel are more important than one's own life.

The title "Son of God" was seen as the supreme Christological title for Jesus in Mark's Gospel. Against its Old Testament background, this term denotes primarily a unique moral and functional relationship to God. Mark reinterprets the title "Son of God," as he did with the title "Christ," to fit into his primary focus on suffering. The Christological highpoint of the Gospel is reached when the centurion recognizes the dead body of the crucified Jesus as the Son of God (15:39). According to Mark, the place to perceive Jesus' Sonship is not first of all in glory, but in his suffering and death. This was foreshadowed at the baptism when Jesus identified with the poor broken, sinful people coming to be baptized. Mark identifies Jesus as the Son of God, and then proceeds to define this title in terms of the Suffering Servant. The implications of Jesus' designation as the Son of God for discipleship are clear when one examines the new family texts of 3:35 and 10:29-30. Jesus is God's Son, and those who do God's will are brother, sister, and mother of Jesus (3:35). Just as the Son of God is obedient to the will of God, so must those he calls brother, sister, and mother be obedient to God's will.

In the Old Testament "son of man" is used to refer to human beings in general, a specific human being, and to an apocalyptic figure who will come with the clouds of heaven and be given power, glory and the Kingdom. While Mark does include several future apocalyptic sayings in the Gospel, he appears most interested in those Son of Man sayings which refer to the humiliation, suffering, and death of Jesus. In all three passion-resurrection predictions Jesus tells us that it is necessary for the Son of Man to suffer, die, and rise. The implications of this title for discipleship are clear when Jesus says that "the Son of Man also came not to be served but to serve, and to give his life as a ransom for many" (10:45). The model for the Christian disciple, and the church, is the suffering service of Jesus.

Mark 10:45 is important not just because the title Son of Man appears there, but because the phrase "a ransom for many" alludes to Isaiah 53:10-12. Although the title "Servant of the Lord" does not occur in Mark's Gospel, it is clear that this figure also plays an important role in shaping Mark's picture of Jesus. The importance of Isaiah 42:1ff. for the baptism scene and Isaiah 52:13–53:12 for the passion narrative is obvious. The point, of course, is not merely Jesus' identity, but instruction for the disciples in service. Mark has Jesus present suffering servanthood as a model for the disciples to follow in 10:45, just as he tells them to take up their crosses after the first passion-resurrection prediction (8:34) and to be servants of all after the second passion-resurrection prediction (9:35).

Jesus calls his disciples to follow him. According to Mark, therefore, the way of the Christian disciple must be the way of the Messiah, the Son of Man, the Son of God. But Mark explains each of these Christological titles in such a way that, in the final analysis, the way of discipleship is the way of the Suffering Servant.

8

The Importance of Mark for Us Today

Mark tells us that the reign of God has come in the person and ministry of Jesus: "The time is fulfilled, and the Kingdom of God is at hand; repent, and believe in the gospel" (1:15). The eschatological hope of Israel is now being fulfilled; the eternal kingship of God is being manifest now, in this world. The one whose arrival Israel has awaited for centuries, the Messiah, the son of David, the king of Israel, has come. Instead of the final world-ending display of divine power that Israel had expected, however, has come the inbreaking of the final era. God is beginning to rule the world in a fuller sense than he had before, but there is still a future dimension to his Kingdom. The reign of God is already here, but the Kingdom has not yet manifested itself in its fullness. In the present, therefore, the Kingdom remains hidden.

Because the Kingdom is now present, it is possible for individuals, through the grace of God, to participate in his reign. But because the Kingdom is now hidden, not here in its eschatological fullness, both repentance and faith are necessary. In spite of the fact that the reign of God has begun, it is still possible for individuals to fail. Those who acknowledge the present reality of God's rule and order their lives in accordance with God's will are the ones who already participate in the present yet hidden Kingdom of God.

The expressions "Kingdom of God" and "reign of God" both suggest a realm or community in which God's rule is exercised. While the Kingdom and the church are not identical, they are intimately related. For those who are called to Christian discipleship, therefore, submitting to God's will means following the way of Jesus, which includes participating in the new type of human community made possible by the arrival of the Kingdom of God. Those who "repent and believe in the gospel" constitute the present manifestation of this community and are promised entrance into the Kingdom when it comes in its fullness. According to Mark, an essential part of Christian discipleship is that those individuals whom Jesus has called to follow him become a visible community. They are distinguished by the fact that they are the brothers and sisters of Jesus who practice baptism and join together for the communal celebration of the Eucharist.

The appropriate response of individuals today is the same as it was when Mark wrote his Gospel. Like the original readers of this Gospel, we too live in the time between the arrival of the Kingdom and its coming in fullness when the Son of Man returns with "great power and glory." The reign of God which came in the person and work of Jesus remains today a present yet hidden reality. Individuals both outside and inside the Christian community are still called upon to "repent and believe in the gospel." For the community gathered in Jesus' name is the primary location where the grace of God manifests itself as love and reconciliation.

In the Gospel, Mark teaches his readers what the call to discipleship, to follow the path of Jesus, actually entails. But is this teaching about discipleship addressed to all or to just a few? A number of years ago it was fashionable to claim that the Gospels taught a two-level ethic, one standard for the elite, priests and religious, and another easier standard for the average person, the laity. The result of this two-level ethic, of course, was to create a class of leaders who could hold up themselves and their way of life as superior to that of the ordinary Christian. The laity were seen as deficient, especially in the area of sexuality, and never able to become perfect like their leaders. Echoes of this earlier position are sometimes found even today. Occasionally someone will claim that celibacy is a more perfect expression of Christian discipleship than marriage. Sometimes lay people accept the two-level ethic because it allows them to ignore the demands of the Gospel. They find comfort in claiming that the teachings of Scripture are meant to be taken seriously only by the elite. Under this two-level ethic the radical demands of the Gospel were seen as addressed only to "the Twelve" and their successors (understood as the clergy). The church's emphasis that its leaders, seen as successors to the apostles, be male and celibate inevitably made it easy for some to conclude that little if any of the New Testament's ethical teaching applied to themselves. What appears at first to be somewhat comforting, that there are no high standards one must try to attain, actually has the effect of confirming the second-class status of these Christians.

Mark does not allow us to arrive at such conclusions. It is widely recognized today that Jesus does not teach a two-level ethic and that there is no hint of a two-level ethic in Mark's Gospel. On the contrary, because the Twelve are presented as symbolic of all disciples, what is required of them is expected of all. This means that members of the laity are no longer relegated to the position of second-rate Christians, but neither are they able to feel comfortable with any half-hearted attempt to fulfill the demands of the Gospel. The radical teachings of Jesus are addressed to all who would be his followers. We must also note that Mark does not teach us in his Gospel either that celibacy is superior to the married life, or that the "religious" life is superior to that of the lay person, or that male followers of Jesus are superior to female disciples. What he does picture is an egalitarian community in which all who do the will of God are brothers and sisters of Jesus and in which the Gentile-like exercise of power and authority is prohibited.

While Mark tells us explicitly only about the call of Jewish men, it is clear that he counts women and non-Jewish men among the disciples of Jesus. Although infant baptism is not dealt with explicitly, children are used as models of discipleship and appear to be seen as members of the Christian community.

The call to follow Jesus includes, as was mentioned above, an invitation to become a member of the community of Jesus' followers which we refer to as the church. Mark's picture of Jesus as the great unifier and of the church as inclusive and not exclusive has significance for us today when we examine how minorities are treated within the church. Mark teaches us that there should be no racial, sexual, economic, or age discrimination in the church.

The equality we have been speaking about is also apparent in Jesus' teaching on marriage and divorce. Although the Jewish Law permitted a man to issue a bill of divorce to his wife, Mark teaches that this is not in agreement with God's will. According to Mark neither spouse should divorce the other. At the very least, this rules out for Christians any cavalier attitude toward divorce and demands that marriage be taken quite seriously. While Mark does not have the final word on marriage and divorce in the New Testament, his understanding of the teaching of Jesus on this matter cannot be ignored.

We saw earlier that the call to follow Jesus is a call to conversion of life, obedience, trust and hope. Mark calls for all Christians honestly to assess the status of their commitment to the person and work of Jesus. Many who emphasize trust or hope would do well to consider Mark's emphasis on doing, not just hearing, the will of God. Others who have turned discipleship into a kind of legalism, emphasizing obedience above all else, would do well to consider the Gospel's emphasis on "believing," on trust and on hope.

In our examination of the call stories we concluded that the call to follow Jesus carried with it a missionary charge. Many Christians would undoubtedly agree that the missionary enterprise is an important part of discipleship, yet assign this task to others within the church. Frequently mission is seen as a corporate responsibility, but not an individual responsibility. Mark does not support this interpretation as many different individuals in his Gospel proclaim the good news. Thus, Mark presents us with the opportunity to discuss how we as individual Christians can fulfill this missionary charge in our own lives.

Elsewhere in the New Testament we learn that it is baptism which visibly incorporates us into the Body of Christ, the church, and the celebration of the Eucharist which serves as the central celebration of this community as it recalls the life, death, and resurrection of Jesus. Both baptism and the Eucharist are presented in Mark's Gospel in such a way that they are obviously accepted as important in Mark's community. The gathering together of the Christian community for support, encouragement, and nourishment was taken for granted in the early church.

We must follow Mark and emphasize the communal nature of Christianity. Far too many modern Christians fail to see other followers of Jesus as their brothers and sisters. We must all share the blame for this. Most people find it much harder to ignore the needs of a friend or relative than those of a stranger. The obvious conclusion is that if one starts to see the other members of the Christian community as one's brothers and sisters in Christ, then a greater responsibility for their welfare ensues. It is simply easier, more convenient, not to get involved. This selfishness and irresponsibility previously found support in the now defunct two-level ethic. Church leaders too share the blame. Many have done little or nothing to foster this sense of community because they see the more active role of the laity as threatening to their own power and authority. It should be obvious to all that this egocentric attitude on the part of clergy and laity alike is not in agreement with the teachings of Jesus.

The realization that we are all brothers and sisters should lead us, as members of this new community, to adopt an unselfish, sharing lifestyle. It should result in more active involvement in and commitment to the community and its members. The discovery of the communal nature of discipleship also should lead the follower of Jesus to adopt a new attitude toward personal possessions. Mark's comments on the incompatibility of wealth and discipleship will have new meaning when we realize that these words are addressed to all Christians, not just the so-called elite. Our lives will forever change once we accept the fact that we have a responsibility for the spiritual and economic well-being of our brothers and sisters.

Mark tells us quite clearly that the way of Jesus is not the way of selfishness. In the modern world this means, among other things, that Christians will have to ask themselves some very difficult questions about the compatibility between their wealth and their claim to be disciples of Jesus. It is true that the point of several Markan pericopes is that one must let nothing stand in the way of one's commitment to Jesus, neither possessions nor family nor occupation. The story of the rich man is thus understood as teaching that egoism must cease and neither possessions nor the desire for them must stop one from following Jesus. To conclude that Jesus is merely demanding total submission to himself, however, is to miss the undeniable fact that wealth and possessions are the most common idols of those who live in the so-called First World. We are constantly being urged to choose affluence and the security it is said to promise instead of a lifestyle in which our possessions are placed at the service of those in need.

While Mark does not teach that one must physically abandon all one's possessions in order to follow Jesus, neither does he specifically state how much one can retain. Although the terms "rich" and "poor" are relative, it is clear that what remains after one has satisfied the basic needs of life (i.e., food, clothing, and shelter) is what makes one rich. When the entire global community is taken into consideration, it is also clear that most residents of the First World have a disproportionate amount left over after these basic needs are met. Modern Christians must look at their own economic situation in light of Mark's Gospel and decide if their present affluence can be justified. With so many poor and needy at home and throughout the world, perhaps it is time to simplify the way we live. We must also become advocates of the poor and oppose political and economic systems that perpetuate social injustices. Christians will have to declare openly and publicly that property rights are not absolute. The right of individuals and governments to use land and resources as they please must be seen as subordinate to the right of all people to eat and to earn a just living. Mark's Gospel challenges us to reassess our lifestyle and to take the steps necessary to restructure our lives in accordance with the will of God.

Mark's picture of the early Christian community and Jesus' negative assessment concerning the ways the Gentiles govern also have important implications for today's church. Two observations are in order: (1) The way of the world in the late twentieth century is not much different in this respect from the Greco-Roman world in which Jesus lived. All too frequently we are provided with examples of the abuse of power and authority. As in the days of Jesus, this usually involves the selfishness of the powerful elite and the exploitation of the poor and marginalized. (2) Some would suggest that the church of the late twentieth century resembles too closely the world in which it lives in the way its leaders exercise power and authority. All of us, especially those with authority, must examine our behavior in light of Jesus' words and Mark's picture of an egalitarian church.

This self examination must also include a personal response to Jesus' question, "Who do you say that I am?" Mark has told us that Jesus is the Messiah, the son of David, and the king of Israel. But he has also informed us that Jesus is the Son of God and the suffering, dying, rising Son of Man. As the church reflected on the Christ event, in the years leading up to the Council of Nicea and beyond, the most important Christological title for Jesus in Mark's Gospel, Son of God, was seen to include even more than Mark intended. Sometimes this emphasis on the divinity of Jesus has resulted in a triumphalist Christology in which Christians ignore the suffering and death of Jesus. If one considers this aspect of Jesus' ministry unimportant, then in all likelihood the commands to be a servant/slave of all and to pick up one's cross and follow Jesus are also seen as irrelevant. Mark's obvious insistence on the importance of this theme suggests that to ignore it would be an enormous mistake.

The fact that Mark understands Jesus as commissioned to fulfill the task of the Suffering Servant is significant for any modern discussion of the appropriate Christian attitude toward the use of violence. Jesus' insistence on renouncing violence is expressed most clearly by Matthew and Luke, but Mark's understanding of Jesus as the Suffering Servant who "had done no violence" (Isaiah 53:9) allows us to arrive at the same conclusion. As Christians we are called to take up our cross and follow Jesus. The presence of the Kingdom of God requires Christians, with the help of God's grace, to conform their lives to the will of God. The followers of Jesus, the Suffering Servant, are not to impose their will on anyone by force. The way the Gentiles use power and authority is an acceptable model for dealing neither with inner community matters nor with those outside the community. Christians should prefer to suffer injustice themselves rather than impose their rights on others through the use of violence. We would all do well to assess our own lives and our use of any power we might have. Jesus, the Suffering Servant, the Son of God has given us an example to follow. We must take up our cross and follow him, ready to lose our life if necessary, in the nonviolent service of the gospel. In both word and deed, Jesus tells us that discipleship means to serve, not to be served.

Bibliography

Achtemeier, P. J. "An Exposition of Mark 9:30-37." *Int* 30 (1976) 178-183.

_____. "Gospel Miracle Tradition and the Divine Man." *Int* 26 (1972) 174-197.

_____. "'And He Followed Him': Miracles and Discipleship in Mark 10:46-52." *Semeia* 11 (1978) 115-145.

_____ "'He Taught Them Many Things': Reflections on Marcan Christology." *CBQ* 42 (1980) 465-481.

_____. *Invitation to Mark.* Garden City: Doubleday, 1978.

_____. *Mark.* 2nd ed., Proclamation Commentaries. Philadelphia: Fortress, 1986.

_____. "Mark as Interpreter of the Jesus Traditions." *Int* 32 (1978) 339-352.

_____. "The Origin and Function of the Pre-Markan Miracle Catenae." *JBL* 91 (1972) 198-221.

Ambrozic, A.M. *The Hidden Kingdom.* CBQMS 2. Washington, DC: The Catholic Biblical Association of America, 1972.

Au, W. "Discipleship in Mark." *TBT* 67 (1973) 1249-1251.

Baab, O. J. "Father." *IDB* 2, 245.

Bamburger, B. J. "Tax Collector." *IDB* 4, 522.

Barrett, C. K. "The Background of Mark 10:45." In *New Testament Essays: Studies in Memory of T. W. Manson*, ed. A. J. B. Higgins. Manchester: Manchester University, 1959.

Beasley-Murray, G. R. *Baptism in the New Testament*. Grand Rapids: Eerdmans, 1962.

Beck, N. A. "Reclaiming a Biblical Text: The Mark 8:14-21 Discussion about Bread in the Boat." *CBQ* 43 (1981) 49-56.

Behm, J. and E. Würthwein. "*μετανοέω* and *μετάνοια*." *TDNT* 4, 975-1006.

Best, E. "The Camel and the Needle's Eye (MK 10:25)." *ExpTim* 82 (1970-71) 83-89.

_____. *Following Jesus: Discipleship in the Gospel of Mark*. JSNTSup 4. Sheffield: JSOT, 1981.

_____. "Mark's Use of the Twelve." *ZNW* 69 (1978) 11-35.

_____. "The Role of the Disciples in Mark." *NTS* 23 (1976-77) 377-401.

Betz, H. D. *Nachfolge und Nachahmung Jesu Christi im Neuen Testament*. BHT 37. Tübingen: Mohr/Siebeck, 1967.

Betz, O. "The Concept of the So-Called 'Divine-Man' in Mark's Christology." In *Studies in New Testament and Early Christian Literature*. NovTSup 33. ed. D.E. Aune, Leiden: Brill, 1972.

Beyer, H. W. "*διακονέω*." *TDNT* 2, 81-93.

Black, M. "The Christological Use of the Old Testament in the New Testament." *NTS* 18 (1971/72) 1-14.

Bonhoeffer, D. *The Cost of Discipleship*, rev. ed. trans. R. H. Fuller. New York: Macmillan, 1963.

Boomershine, T. E. "Mark 16:8 and the Apostolic Commission." *JBL* 100 (1981) 225-239.

Bornkamm, G. *Jesus of Nazareth*. Trans. I. and F. McLuskey. New York: Harper, 1961.

Braaten, C. E. *The Future of God*. New York: Harper & Row, 1969.

Brandon, S. G. F. *Jesus and the Zealots*. New York: Scribner's, 1967.

Brown, R., et al. *Mary in the New Testament*. Philadelphia: Fortress; New York: Paulist, 1978.

_____. *Peter in the New Testament*. Minneapolis: Augsburg; New York: Paulist, 1973.

Bultmann, R. *History of the Synoptic Tradition*. 3rd ed. trans. J. Marsh. New York: Harper & Row, 1963.

_____ and A. Weiser, "πιστεύω." *TDNT* 6, 174-228.

Carlston, C. E. *The Parables of the Triple Tradition*. Philadelphia: Fortress, 1975.

Catchpole, D. "Discipleship, The Law, and Jesus of Nazareth." *Crux* 11 (1973) 8-16.

Cullmann, O. *Baptism in the New Testament*. London: SCM, 1950.

_____. *The Christology of the New Testament*. Trans. S.C. Guthrie and C. A. M. Hall. Philadelphia: Westminster, 1959.

Dahl, N. A. "The Parables of Growth." *ST* 5 (1952) 132-166.

Davis, W. D. "Reflections on a Scandinavian Approach to the Gospel Tradition.'" In *Neotestamentica et Patristica: Freundsgabe Oscar Cullmann*. NovTSup 6. Leiden: Brill, 1962.

Dewey, J. *Disciples of the Way: Mark on Discipleship*. Cincinnati: Women's Division, Board of Global Ministries, The United Methodist Church, 1976.

Dodd, C. H. *According to the Scriptures*. New York: Scribner's, 1953.

_____. "The Kingdom of God Has Come." *ExpTim* 48 (1936-37) 138-142.

_____. *The Parables of the Kingdom.* Rev. ed. New York: Scribner's, 1961.

Donahue, J. R. *Are You The Christ?* SBLDS 10. Missoula: University of Montana, 1973.

_____. "Introduction: From Passion Traditions to Passion Narrative." In *The Passion in Mark*, ed. W.H. Kelber. Philadelphia: Fortress, 1976.

_____. "A Neglected Factor in the Theology of Mark." *JBL* 101 (1982) 563-594.

_____. "Temple, Trial, and Royal Christology (Mark 14:53-65)." In *The Passion in Mark*, ed. W. H. Kelber. Philadelphia: Fortress, 1976.

_____. *The Theology and Setting of Discipleship in the Gospel of Mark.* The 1983 Pere Marquette Theology Lecture. Milwaukee: Marquette University, 1983.

Donaldson, J. "'Called to Follow.' A Twofold Experience of Discipleship in Mark." *BTB* 5 (1975) 67-77.

Dulles, A. "The Meaning of Faith Considered in Relationship to Justice." In *The Faith That Does Justice*, ed. J. C. Haughey. New York: Paulist, 1977.

Estrada Díaz, J. A. "Las relaciones Jesús-pueblo-discípulos en el evangelio de Marcos." *Estudios Eclesiásticos* 54 (1979) 151-170.

Feuillet, A. The Baptism of Jesus." *TD* 14 (1966) 207-212.

Fiorenza, E. Schüssler. *In Memory of Her.* New York: Crossroad, 1983.

Fitzmyer, J. A. *The Gospel According to Luke I-IX.* Garden City: Doubleday, 1981.

_____. *A Wandering Aramean.* SBLMS 25. Missoula: Scholars, 1979.

Fleddermann, H. "The Discipleship Discourse (Mark 9:33-50)." *CBQ* 43 (1981) 57-75.

Fletcher, D. R. "Condemned to Die." *Int* 18 (1964) 156-164.

Ford, J. M. *My Enemy Is My Guest.* Maryknoll: Orbis, 1984.

Fowler, R. M. *Loaves and Fishes.* SBLDS 54. Ann Arbor: Edwards Brothers, 1981.

Freyne, S. *The Twelve: Disciples and Apostles.* London: Sheed and Ward, 1968.

Fuller, R. H. *The Foundations of New Testament Christology.* New York: Scribner's, 1965.

_____ and P. Perkins. *Who Is This Christ?* Philadelphia: Fortress, 1983.

Gerhardsson, B. *Memory and Manuscript.* ASNU 22. Lund: Gleerup, 1961.

Grassi, J. A. "The Eucharist in the Gospel of Mark." *AER* 168 (1974) 595-608.

Griffiths, J. G. "The Disciple's Cross" *NTS* 16 (1970) 358-364.

Hahn, F. *The Titles of Jesus in Christology.* New York: World, 1969.

Hamburger, H. "Money, Coins." *IDB* 3, 423-435.

Hay, L. S. "The Son-of-God Christology in Mark." *JBR* 32 (1964) 106-114.

Hengel, M. *The Charismatic Leader and His Followers.* Trans. J. Greig. New York: Crossroad, 1981.

_____. "The Gospel of Mark: Time of Origin and Situation." In *Studies in the Gospel of Mark.* Trans. J. Bowden. Philadelphia: Fortress, 1985.

Higgins, A. J. B. *Jesus and the Son of Man.* Philadelphia: Fortress, 1964.

_____. *The Son of Man in the Teaching of Jesus.* SNTSMS 39. Cambridge: Cambridge University, 1980.

Hinnebusch, P. *Jesus, The New Elijah.* Ann Arbor: Servant, 1978.

Holladay, C. R. *Theios Anēr in Hellenistic Judaism: A Critique of the Use of this Category in New Testament Christology.* SBLDS 40. Missoula: Scholars, 1977.

Jeremias, J. *Infant Baptism in the First Four Centuries.* Trans. D. Cairns. Philadelphia: Westminster, 1960.

_____. *The Parables of Jesus.* Rev. ed. trans. S. Hooke. New York: Scribner's 1963.

Kasper, W. *Theology of Christian Marriage.* Trans. D. Smith. New York: Crossroad, 1983.

Keck, L. E. "The Introduction to Mark's Gospel." *NTS* 12 (1966) 352-370.

Kee, H. *Community of the New Age: Studies in Mark's Gospel.* Philadelphia: Westminster, 1977.

Kelber, W. H. "Apostolic Tradition and the Form of the Gospel." In *Discipleship in the New Testament*, ed. F.F. Segovia. Philadelphia: Fortress, 1985.

_____. "The Hour of the Son of Man and the Temptation of the Disciples (Mark 14:32-42)." In *The Passion in Mark*, ed. W. H. Kelber. Philadelphia: Fortress, 1976.

_____. *The Kingdom in Mark: A New Place and A New Time.* Philadelphia: Fortress, 1974.

_____. "Mark 14:32-42: Gethsemane." *ZNW* 63 (1972) 166-187.

_____. *Mark's Story of Jesus.* Philadelphia: Fortress, 1979.

_____. *The Oral and Written Gospel: The Hermeneutics of Speaking and Writing in the Synoptic Tradition, Mark, Paul, and Q.* Philadelphia: Fortress, 1983.

_____. ed. *The Passion in Mark.* Philadelphia: Fortress, 1976.

Kingsbury, J. D. *The Christology of Mark's Gospel.* Philadelphia: Fortress, 1983.

Kirby, M. F. "Mark's Prerequisite for Being an Apostle." *TBT* 18 (1980) 77-81.

Kittel, G. "'ακολουθέω." *TDNT* 1, 210-216.

Kraybill, D. B. and Sweetland, D. M. "Possessions in Luke-Acts: A Sociological Perspective." *PRS* 10 (1983) 215-239.

Kuby, A. "Zur Konzeption des Markus-Evangeliums." *ZNW* 49 (1958) 52-64.

Lane, W. L. "Theios *Anēr,* Christology and the Gospel of Mark." In *New Dimensions in New Testament Study*, ed. R. N. Longenecker and M. C. Tenney. Grand Rapids: Zondervan, 1974.

Lindars, B. *New Testament Apologetics.* Philadelphia: Westminster, 1961.

Lohfink, G. *Jesus and Community.* Trans. J. P. Galvin. Philadelphia: Fortress, 1984.

Luccock, H. E. "The Gospel According to St. Mark." *IB* 7, 627-917.

Malone, D. "Riches and Discipleship: Mark 10:23-31." *BTB* 9 (1979) 78-88.

Manno, B. V. "The Identity of Jesus and Christian Discipleship in the Gospel of Mark." *Religious Education* 70 (1975) 619-628.

Marshall, I. H. "Son of God or Servant of Yahweh? — A Reconsideration of Mark 1:11." *NTS* 15 (1968) 326-336.

Marxsen, W. *The Lord's Supper as a Christological Problem.* Trans. L. Nieting. Philadelphia: Fortress, 1970.

Matera, F. J. *The Kingship of Jesus: Composition and Theology in Mark 15.* SBLDS 66. Chico: Scholars, 1982.

Metzger, B. M. *A Textual Commentary on the Greek New Testament.* New York: United Bible Societies, 1971.

Meye, R. P. *Jesus and the Twelve: Discipleship and Revelation in Mark's Gospel.* Grand Rapids: Eerdmans, 1968.

Michel, O. "*κάμηλος.*" *TDNT* 3, 592-594.

Minear, P. S. *Commands of Christ.* Nashville: Abingdon, 1972.

Moule, C. F. D. *The Origins of Christology.* Cambridge: Cambridge University, 1977.

Munro, W. "Women Disciples in Mark?" *CBQ* 44 (1982) 225-241.

Murphy, C. M. "Discipleship in Mark as Movement with Christ." *TBT* 53 (1971) 305-308.

Murray, D. J. "Mark's Theology of Baptism." *Dimension* 8 (1976) 92-97.

Neusner, J. *First-Century Judaism in Crisis.* Nashville: Abingdon, 1975.

Nineham, D. E. *Saint Mark.* Pelican Gospel Commentaries. Baltimore: Penguin, 1963.

O'Toole, R. F. *The Unity of Luke's Theology.* Wilmington: Michael Glazier, 1984.

Pannenberg, W. *Theology and the Kingdom of God.* Philadelphia: Westminster, 1969.

Parker, P. "Crucifixion." *IDB* 1, 746-747.

Peacock, H. F. "Discipleship in the Gospel of Mark." *RevExp* 75 (1978) 555-564.

Perrin, N. "The High Priest's Question and Jesus' Answer (Mark 14:61-62)." In *The Passion in Mark*, ed. W. H. Kelber. Philadelphia: Fortress, 1976.

_____. *A Modern Pilgrimage in New Testament Christology.* Philadelphia: Fortress, 1974.

_____. *The New Testament: An Introduction.* 2nd ed. N. Perrin and D. C. Duling. New York: Harcourt, Brace, Jovanovich, 1982.

_____. *The Resurrection According to Matthew, Mark, and Luke.* Philadelphia: Fortress, 1977.

_____. *What is Redaction Criticism?* Philadelphia: Fortress, 1969.

Pesch, R. *Das Markusevangelium.* HTKNT 2. Freiburg/ Basel/Wien: Herder, 1976-1977.

Petersen, N.R. *Literary Criticism for New Testament Critics.* GBS. Philadelphia: Fortress, 1978.

Pope, M.H. "Seven, Seventh, Seventy." *IDB* 4, 294-295.

Pudussery, P.S. "The Meaning of Discipleship in the Gospel of Mark." *Jeevadhara* 10 (1980) 93-110.

Quesnell, Q. *The Mind of Mark.* Rome: Pontifical Biblical Institute, 1969.

Rahner, K. "Church and World." *Encyclopedia of Theology.* New York: Seabury, 1975.

Rengstorff, K.H. "*διδάσκω.*" *TDNT* 2, 135-148.

_____. "*δοῦλος.*" *TDNT* 2, 261-280.

_____. "*μαθητής.*" *TDNT* 4, 415-459.

Reumann, J. *Jesus In The Church's Gospels.* Philadelphia: Fortress, 1968.

Riga, P.J. "Poverty as Counsel and as Precept." *TBT* 65 (1973) 1123-1128.

Rigaux. B. *The Testimony of St. Mark.* Chicago: Franciscan Herald, 1966.

Robbins, V.K. "Last Meal: Preparation, Betrayal, and Absence (Mark 14:12-25)." In *The Passion in Mark,* ed. W.H. Kelber. Philadelphia: Fortress, 1976.

_____. "Summons and Outline in Mark: The Three-Step Progression." *NovT* 23 (1981) 97-114.

Ruppert, L. *Jesus als der leidende Gerechte.* SBS 59. Stuttgart: Katholisches Bibelwerk, 1972.

Schmahl, G. *Die Zwölf im Markusevangelium: Eine redaktionsgeschichtliche Untersuchung.* TTS 30. Trier: Paulinus, 1974.

Schnackenburg, R. *Das Evangelium nach Markus.* Düsseldorf: Patmos, 1966.

Schottroff, L. and Stegemann, W. *Jesus von Nazareth. Hoffnung der Armen.* Stuttgart: Kohlhammer, 1978.

Schulz, A. *Nachfolgen und Nachahmen. Studien über das Verhältnis der neutestamentlichen Jüngerschaft zur urchristlichen Vorbildethik.* SANT 6. Munich: Kösel, 1962.

Schweizer, E. *The Good News According to Mark.* Trans. D. Madvig. Richmond: John Knox, 1970.

_____. *Lordship and Discipleship.* SBT 28. Naperville: Allenson, 1960.

_____. "The Portrayal of the Life of Faith in the Gospel of Mark." *Int* 32 (1978) 387-399.

Selvidge, M.J. "'And Those Who Followed Feared' (Mark 10:32)." *CBQ* 45 (1983) 396-400.

Smith, C.W.F. "Prayer." *IDB* 3, 857-867.

Smith, M. "A Comparison of Early Christian and Early Rabbinic Tradition." *JBL* 82 (1963) 169-176.

Stock, A. *Call to Discipleship: A Literary Study of Mark's Gospel.* Wilmington: Michael Glazier, 1982.

Stock, K. *Boten aus dem Mit-Ihm-Sein: Das Verhältnis zwischen Jesus und den Zwölf nach Markus.* AnBib 70. Rome Biblical Institute, 1975.

Talbert, C.H. *Reading Luke*. New York: Crossroad, 1984.

Tannehill, R.C. "The Disciples in Mark: The Function of a Narrative Role" *JR* 57 (1977) 386-405.

_____. "The Gospel of Mark as Narrative Christology." *Semeia* 16 (1979) 57-95.

Taylor, V. *The Gospel According to St. Mark*. 2nd ed. London: Macmillan, 1966.

_____. *The Names of Jesus*. New York: St. Martin's, 1953.

Tödt, H.E. *The Son of Man In The Synoptic Tradition*. Philadelphia: Westminster, 1965.

Turner, C.H. "Markan Usages VIII: The Disciples and the Twelve." *JTS* 28 (1926-27) 22-30.

Tyson, J.B. "The Blindness of the Disciples in Mark." *JBL* 80 (1961) 261-268.

van Iersel, B. "Die wunderbare Speisung und das Abendmahl in der synoptischen Tradition." *NovT* 7 (1964) 167-194.

Van Cangh, J.-M. *La Multiplication des pains et l'Eucharistie*. Paris: Cerf, 1975.

Vermes, G. *Jesus the Jew*. New York: Macmillan, 1973.

Weeden, T.J. "The Heresy That Necessitated Mark's Gospel." *ZNW* 59 (1968) 145-158.

_____*Mark: Traditions in Conflict*. Philadelphia: Fortress, 1971.

Wright, A.G. "The Widow's Mite: Praise or Lament? A Matter of Context." *CBQ* 44 (1982) 256-265.

Zimmerli, W. and J. Jeremias. "παῖς θεοῦ." *TDNT* 5, 654-717.

_____. *The Servant of God*. SBT 20. London: SCM, 1965.

Index of Authors

Index of Scripture References

Old Testament

Intertestamental Literature

New Testament